Russell Lynes

A

SURFEIT

OF

HONEY

Harper & Brothers Publishers New York

A friendly, if somewhat skeptical, excursion into the manners and customs of Americans in this time of prosperity.

H | B

Books by Russell Lynes:

A SURFEIT OF HONEY

THE TASTEMAKERS

GUESTS

SNOBS

A Surfeit of Honey

A SURFEIT OF HONEY

Copyright *1953, 1954, 1955, 1956, 1957 by Russell Lynes*

Printed in the United States of America

FIRST EDITION

L-F

Library of Congress catalog card number: 56-11078

Soc. Sci
hist
2. 4-57

Contents

They surfeited with honey and began
To loathe the taste of sweetness, whereof a little
More than a little is by much too much.

King Henry the Fourth, Part One

ACKNOWLEDGMENTS

Parts of several chapters of this book have been published in *Harper's Magazine*, *McCall's*, *Look*, and *Mademoiselle*, and I should like to thank their editors for giving me permission to reprint them here. I am especially indebted to Katherine Gauss Jackson and Eric Larrabee for their invaluable advice, to Virginia Hughes and Elizabeth R. Lynes for their help with the preparation of the manuscript and for suggestions, and to David Riesman for permission to quote from his article in *The American Scholar*. I should also like to thank my colleagues on *Harper's Magazine*, and most particularly John Fischer, for making it possible for me to take time from my editorial duties to work on this book.

R. L.

A Surfeit of Honey

Chapter I

The Baron's Castle

WHEN Dr. Ernest Jones, a distinguished psychoanalyst and Freud's biographer and friend, arrived in New York. from his home in London after a long absence, a newspaper reporter asked him if he thought that the new tranquilizing drugs were a cure-all.

"Cure everything?" Dr. Jones replied. "Cure politics?"

Ours is a society with more built-in tranquilizers of more different sorts than any that has ever existed, and if they have not cured politics, they have certainly dulled a great many people's interest in them. We have provided ourselves with cushions and anxiety relievers in every corner of the room, so that if we should stumble, by any chance, we will be sure to land without bruises—cushions of social security, of leisure, of gadgets, of pensions and plans against every sort of evil day. What we have not managed to legislate into shock absorbers we have taken care of with inventions which either keep us busy or keep us lulled. For every increase in speed we have found a counter-irritant of slowness. To offset the four-hundred-mile-an-hour jet transport we have jammed the roads to the airports with traffic. For every got-to-get-there we have a take-it-easy. Executives come with built-in ulcers. Two hundred-and-forty-horsepower cars come with built-in safety belts.

We are the only modern nation that has, since the Second World War, got almost everything that it has asked for—and a good deal else besides. We have, as a result, changed tremendously in many ways, in our attitudes toward the good life, in our relations to each other and to people abroad, and in our assessments of success and failure. We have got power, which we did not especially want because of the responsibilities that go with it, and we have got prosperity, which we wanted with all our hearts. America has in many respects become "the Baron's Castle."

In *Candide*, you may remember, Voltaire introduces the incorrigibly optimistic Dr. Pangloss, professor of practically everything and the retainer of a baron whose wife was a three-hundred-pound baroness, with this sentence: "He proved admirably that there is no effect without

a cause, and that, in this best of all possible worlds, the Baron's castle was the most magnificent of castles, and his lady the best of all possible Baronesses."

To nearly every American America is the best of all possible lands and his wife is the best of all possible ladies. His world, though there are moments when it seems to be slightly out of hand, is the best of all possible worlds, for he is, like Dr. Pangloss, an optimist at heart. But for all this he is modest about his personal achievements (whatever he may be about his nation's achievements), eager for the success of others, and generous to a degree which the nationals of other countries suspect of being a little too good to be human, and therefore unreal. His manners are so relaxed and friendly that his good will is often taken for insolence by those who do not understand him. He is hospitable, and he expects hospitality of his own open-handed sort from others. He very much wants to be liked, but even more than that he wants to be understood. It doesn't occur to him that some people don't care whether they understand him or not.

One of the reasons why the American is hard to understand is that he refuses to stay still; he is constantly changing. Just when American society and its customs seem for a moment to be settled, they move over. Flux is a far more natural state in America than permanence. This may make us hard to deal with, but whatever people say about America, and they say a good many rude things, they do not say that it is a bore.

A great many of the changes that have taken place in America in the last decade are obvious to everyone. Americans have moved in great numbers to the suburbs and whole new kinds of communities, the mass-produced suburbs, have sprung up. Television has become a topic of conversation as radio never did, and it has changed the way millions of people use their leisure and generate their vicarious emotions. Automation, about which there is nothing especially new but its name, has become a supposed threat to some of us and a vision of more leisure to others. Wonder drugs have vastly increased the size of the retired population and do-it-yourself has given the eternally busy something better to do, they think, than relax.

And there are other changes, less obvious but, I think, not less important, that have wormed their way into our consciousness so slowly that we have scarcely been aware of them at all. To say that we have been going through a social revolution would be to make the constant process of change in America seem like upheaval, which it is not. It is, if anything, just another manifestation of the adaptability of Americans to the circumstances of the moment and of their natural bent for keeping a fairly orderly house with a minimum of housekeeping.

4 . . .

We have, in fact, piled a good many things in the middle of the room and swept a good many things under the rug, and if the Baron's Castle is not quite so magnificent as Dr. Pangloss and the rest of us make it out to be, the effect is pleasant to its inhabitants. One of the things we have swept under the rug is the old and traditional class system of upper, middle, and lower classes that are easily recognizable. We have evolved, more or less without noticing it, a class structure that is better suited than any we have had before to the fluid society of which we have long boasted. It is one in which money counts less and position and accomplishment count a great deal more.

While we have been doing this we have also shuffled the functions of men and women in a most contrary way, not that it has become difficult to tell which is which, but it has become increasingly difficult to tell who does what and why. Men have taken over women's work and women have taken over men's, and with this shift in jobs there has also been a change in men's preoccupation with concerns, like fashion, which have traditionally been women's affair. The nice division of the sexes (and who is to say it hasn't been nice?) has lost some of its sharpness, and while most men may consider this the result of elaborate maneuvers by women, they must accept more than a little of the responsibility themselves.

The fact is that many of the sharp edges that have made

America the rambunctious and fascinating place it is have been sandpapered into comfortable smoothness. Some others at the same time have become nicked and jagged and worrisome. Some of what we have swept under the rug is going to be there to plague our children. But meanwhile we, the optimists, the happy many, live tranquilized in this best of all possible worlds.

Chapter II

What Became of the Upper Class?

AMERICANS have never been able to abide the word "aristocracy," but until just a few years ago "upper class" was an acceptable enough term. For example, the Bradley Martins, who were so well known in the 1890's, were upper class; no one doubted that, whatever one may have thought of the way they behaved.

We have always had a certain number of aristocrats, men and women who have behaved themselves with uncommon dignity, attained prominence, and seemed to be above political prejudices and party concerns, men in our day like General Marshall and Henry L. Stimson. But our aristocrats have had nothing to do with the dictionary definition of the word or with the European idea of the ruling classes. Aristocracy implies to us the heads that rolled beneath the guillotine; it means snobbishness, idleness and hereditary privilege, the rule of the many by the few or, as Webster's says, by the "best, hence government by a relatively small privileged class." Nothing could be further from the democratic ideal.

But upper class is a term that has only recently been relegated to that special subcellar where we keep unfashionable ideas in case we may want to trot them out again. The late Bradley Martins are in that same subcellar, undoubtedly a good deal the worse for neglect. The Bradley Martins really went too far, though most of their friends didn't think so at the time; what they did was done in a spirit of gaiety and it didn't hurt anybody, though it may have been, to use an old phrase, a little too too.

The story is simply this, and it's not very important:

Mrs. Bradley Martin of New York, London, and Inverness (but principally of New York; she had a town house in London and her husband had a shooting box at Inverness) read with dismay one morning at breakfast in 1896 of the plight of the poor. She was moved to do something about it. It was a time of acute economic depression in America, and she took it upon herself to give a costume ball in order, as she said, "to give impetus to trade." If people needed work,

she was in a position to give them something to keep their hands busy. Mrs. Bradley Martin (she was always referred to by both names) was the wife of a man of leisure. Her husband had inherited a more than comfortable fortune from his father, a self-made lawyer and shrewd investor. The Bradley Martins' position in society was secure; their daughter, Cornelia, had when she was only sixteen made an extremely gratifying match with Lord Craven. The Bradley Martins were (although Mrs. B. M. came from Troy, New York) considered "socially acceptable" even in Mrs. Astor's circle of "four hundred."

Mrs. Bradley Martin's "impetus to trade" cost her and her guests $369,200 (or possibly a million dollars, if equated with the current dollar) and it gave employment not only to dressmakers, costumers, hairdressers, headwaiters, caterers, but to at least one armorer and one college professor. Mr. August Belmont appeared at the ball in a "full suit of steel armor inlaid with gold which cost him $10,000." Another gentleman arrived clad in the costume of an American Indian, the details of which had been authenticated by a Harvard professor. The ballroom of the Waldorf-Astoria, then at the corner of Thirty-fourth Street and Fifth Avenue and famous everywhere for its Peacock Alley, was banked with carloads of orchids, roses, galax leaves and "an almost incredible amount of asparagus vine." Mrs. Bradley Martin in a black velvet train lined with cerise satin stood on a dais while a liveried flunkey announced the names of the guests, together with the exact period and nature of the costume in which each was dressed. The ballroom itself was done up as "a replica of a hall in Versailles."

The newspapers, which in those days devoted a great deal of space to describing in loving detail the parties, costumes, guest lists and menus of Society, had a field day with Mrs. Bradley Martin's ball. The first five pages of the New York *Journal* were devoted entirely to it on the day after the party. Even the London *Daily Mail* regaled its readers with a full, if somewhat wryly amused, account of the ball. But it was the publicity that gave the Bradley Martins their comeuppance. The moralists got after them. In *The Saga of American Society*, where the story of the party is recounted in great detail (and from which I have borrowed), Dixon Wecter writes: "Newspaper editors, clergymen, and college debating societies discussed the heartless extravagance of wealth, and even more effectively the New York authorities more than doubled the city tax assessment of the Bradley Martins." As a result they gave up their home in New York and went to live permanently in London.

It was not the fact that the Bradley Martins were "upper class" that infuriated people: it was because they behaved a little too ostentatiously like our popular notion of aristocrats. There were others a good deal richer and just as pretentious, though in a less public fashion who, far from being

10 . . .

made uncomfortable by public opinion, thrived quietly on it. They built tremendous marble "cottages" at Newport or Lenox which they ornamented with furnishings from European palaces; they built vast greenhouses in which tropical trees produced exotic fruits and flowers for their tables. Terraced lawns stepped down to artificial lakes where swans floated on the surface and speckled trout swam beneath. Streams of water splashed from the bronze mouths of satyrs into wide marble basins; the air smelled of heliotrope, and men with rakes smoothed the pebbled driveways after each visiting carriage.

Such was the life of the upper reaches of the upper class—stately, lavish, formal, and on the whole rather boring. But the upper class was more than just the very rich. It was the less rich, the more prosperous professionals, some doctors, some lawyers, some clergymen (especially Episcopal bishops who were actually called "my lord" when visiting in England), and some businessmen. People in trade, unless they reached the prominence of John Wanamaker, were generally thought not to be members of the upper class no matter how much money they made. A few college professors, if they married rich wives, were upper class, as were the presidents of Yale, Harvard, and Princeton. A dentist could never be upper class.

The composition of the upper class was always amorphous, and who "belonged" and who didn't was vague in many American minds. We were content to admit, however, that like nations with traditional aristocracies we did have an upper, a middle, and a lower class. Now we have only a middle class. No one today would be so patronizing as to refer to the lower classes. We tried "the common man" for a brief while, but we gave it up. As for the "upper class," whatever a man may think of his position, wealth, and influence, he knows better than to speak of himself and his peers as members of the upper class. The chairman of the board takes pride (or at least he knows there are advantages) in being called by his first name by his factory hands, as Amory Houghton of the Corning Glass Works is called "Am." You would not today, for instance, hear the phrase that was used so often by Republicans in the 1930's, "Roosevelt is a traitor to his class." It would not occur to anyone, whatever his politics, to say that Mr. Stevenson or Governor Harriman were traitors to their class because they have expressed certain sympathetic views on social legislation. "Damn fools," maybe, or "soft in the head," or even in the mouths of the apoplectic, "fellow travelers," but "traitors to their class," never.

For purposes of common parlance we have a classless society, if a society that has only one class, a middle class, can be said to be classless. "The Government issued today a report," said the *New York Times* in April, 1956, "that might be labeled, 'the growth of the middle-class.' . . .

the number of persons with incomes ranging from $4,000 to $50,000 rose steadily from 1950 through 1952. The report also noted the decline in million dollar incomes. . . . Tax returns showing incomes of $1,000,000 or more dropped to 148 in 1952, compared to 171 in 1951 and 219 in 1950." It is not income above a million or below four thousand that makes a man upper or lower class; his income merely makes him rich or poor. We have devised new ways of dividing people up that are just as effective, if a little less insulting. We have workers, white-collar workers, executives (junior and senior), managers and directors. That might be called a power system of classification. Another is lowbrows, middlebrows, and highbrows. Still another is creative and non-creative workers. Women are housewives, working women, or career women. For all our classlessness we keep assigning people to levels.

We have not, however, found a convenient system for assigning them to social levels, Dr. W. Lloyd Warner and his study of social classes to the contrary notwithstanding. He ranged, you'll remember, from upper-uppers to lower-lowers, with upper-lowers and lower-middles, so that society became a seven-layer cake with each layer tasty to the sociologists but a matter of indifference to almost everyone else. If we were to divide American society, baseball fashion, into the infield, the outfield, and the battery we would come somewhat closer to the way it is actually organized. How you classify a man would then become a matter of position rather than of level. I have been told that, when major league baseball teams travel, a very definite class system operates in the order in which they sit in a bus, with the pitchers and catchers up front, the infield in the middle and the outfielders in the back. In operation, however, the "most valuable player" can as easily be a left fielder as a catcher, just as a skilled machinist can be a more important man in a shop than the shop steward or, indeed, the boss. In America we are far more likely to judge a man by the position he occupies (and we differ tremendously in how much importance we attach to different positions) than by the social level he thinks of himself as belonging to.

Those who occupy the most lordly positions in whatever field they may have become prominent have a good deal of influence over the lives of the rest of us. As a result our society, classless or not, produces a remarkable number of men and women who assume the position of aristocrats.

Unlike the aristocratic classes of Europe, which maintain some kind of permanent if uneasy tenure even when their fortunes are impaired, our aristocrats are a highly volatile lot with their feet in quicksands and their heads in storm clouds. The member of today's aristocracy is more than likely to find himself a run-of-the-mill member of the middle class tomorrow, and our middle class is constantly tossing up new and somewhat astonished aristocrats. When,

for example, we lopped off the heads of the moneyed aristocrats like the Bradley Martins with the sharp edge of the
graduated income tax, we produced a very odd and miscellaneous expense-account aristocracy to take its place; when
we more or less laughed out of countenance the old aristocracy of breeding, we nurtured a new one of industrial
tycoons. Just now we are beginning to see the rise of an
entertainment and "communications" (a basket word meaning the business of trying to sell people ideas) aristocracy
which embraces not only the Goldwyns and the Skourases,
the Sarnoffs and Luces, and the Bentons and Bowleses, but
also the cream of the talent that serves them in their movies,
television, radio, publications, and advertising empires.

There is nothing especially new about this manner of
creating a kind of aristocracy in America, but as our way
of living becomes more complex, our demands more and
more specialized, and business is concentrated in fewer and
fewer large corporations, a change has come over our social
structure which, I think, is something quite new.

Instead of being divided horizontally into levels and
strata, as we are used to thinking of it, our society has increasingly become divided vertically. Instead of broad
upper, middle, and lower classes that cut across the society
of the nation like the clear but uneven slices on a geological
model, we now have a series of almost free-standing pyramids, each with its several levels and each one topped by an

aristocracy of its own. It is a far cry from the top of one of these pyramids to the next, and communication between the members of the aristocracies is occasionally difficult, for they not only speak different languages, but their minds are on quite different things. They have different notions of what constitutes success (though they all like money, of course), and their "status symbols," to use a sociologist's term, are as unlike as, say, a swimming pool and an academic hood.

Let me be specific. I have just mentioned the tycoons, the men on top of the big-business pyramid, and the moguls of the communications and entertainment pyramid. To this can be added an intellectual pyramid, another for small business, one for the underworld, one for labor. There is even one for politics in which the aristocrats are not necessarily the men who sit in high offices but those who run the parties and make the candidates. There is still another for sports.

At the top of the intellectual pyramid, to take one that is close to being neat in its organization, there sits a small group of academics with a few novelists, poets, painters, composers, foundation executives, and university presidents who more or less assume charge of the arts and intellectual life of the nation. Shortly after the Second World War there was a rather interesting tussle for power at the top of this particular pyramid when the atomic physicists, glowing with achievement but frightened by the power they had

unleashed, tried to tell the rest of the intellectual world how it should think and how it should run its and other people's business. They did not, you will remember, get very far. The humanists, together with a few scientists who are also humanists, like Robert Oppenheimer, came out on top. (There was a moment when the humanists thought that the scientists were going to get not only all the money but all the students. They did get most of the money but, poor little rich boys, they are now crying for companionship.) Dr. Oppenheimer's clash with a member of the aristocracy of another pyramid, big business, in the person of Admiral Strauss, the chairman of the Atomic Energy Commission, was one of the most spectacular examples of struggle for power between pyramids in recent years. Business backed Strauss almost to a man; the intellectuals were just as solidly behind Oppenheimer. The issue seems to have been only ostensibly "security," though there are scientists who contend that it was a hassle between two factions of physicists—those who backed Teller and those who favored "Oppie."

At the top of the intellectual pyramid the critics and philosophers today have a power that they have not had in the past in America—men like Jacques Barzun, Lionel Trilling, Reinhold Niebuhr, Norbert Wiener, David Riesman, and, of course, Oppenheimer. They outrank the artists and novelists and poets, who are a little afraid of them, and since they are scholars who can also write for the lay reader they outrank most other academics who can (though many insist otherwise) communicate only with their peers. As David Riesman pointed out some time ago (and as *Time* magazine recently reiterated) the position of the intellectual has never been stronger in America than it is today. It is popular among intellectuals to bemoan the fact that nobody pays any attention to them, that they have never before encountered such a wave of anti-intellectualism, and that they are voices crying in a wilderness. But an intellectual without a wilderness is a missionary without a cannibal. The very fact that the intellectuals have attracted such extensive, and often vituperative, criticism from the peers of other pyramids indicates, Riesman points out, not a lack of influence but a recognition of their power in our society.

There is no need to map the intellectual pyramid from its apex to its base, but it is a fairly cohesive world. Somewhere near its top are the purveyors and interpreters of the word—the publishers and editors of the books and the kinds of magazines for which the intellectual writes, and the reviewers. In some respects they stand in the same relationship to the commanding intellectual aristocrats that the vice president in charge of public relations stands to the industrial tycoon—a nozzle through which his eminence and personality are sprayed on the world outside. With these are the managers of the book clubs in neatly stratified ranks,

for the book clubs have recently come to be divided into fairly clear levels of intellectual aspiration. At the top, for example, is the Reader's Subscription, whose judges are Jacques Barzun, Lionel Trilling, and W. H. Auden, and which has a conscientiously developed reputation for selecting books for its members which the highbrow and the upper middlebrow are likely to find on their "must" lists. There are the Seven Arts Book Club and the Book Find Club which recommend less lofty but still fairly specialized books, and the Book of the Month Club for what can loosely be called the "general reader" who likes a varied diet of not too demanding but well-written novels, biographies and histories, with an occasional picture book thrown in as a premium. Some newspaper columnists, like Walter Lippmann, and television commentators, like Ed Murrow, have a recognized standing in the intellectual world, and though Mr. Murrow may actually be at home with the communications aristocracy, he is regarded by the intellectuals as an ambassador to that other court.

The professional educators, especially those who represent the Teachers College point of view, are looked down upon by the intellectual aristocracy in the same way that journalistic popularizers are looked down upon by academics. They may be necessary to get the message to the people, but they are suspected of diluting the truth to make it acceptable to the lowest common denominator of intelligence. If the intellectual pyramid has a lower class, journalists and schoolteachers are it. They constitute the broad base of workers which supports the rest of the structure but which gets little acclaim from the top or from those at the bases of other pyramids where other kinds of workers perform comparable functions. The principal complaint of teachers these days is not that they are paid too little but that they lack standing in the eyes of the community. This may well be because they are patronized and looked down upon (though somewhat affectionately) by the upper reaches of their own kind.

The "status symbols" of the intellectual class are not fine cars, swimming pools, minks, or servants, as they are in some of the other aristocratic groups. They are more likely to be honorary degrees from distinguished universities, a bibliography of articles about themselves by other and lesser members of their own group, and laurels such as the Nobel Prize, of course, and lesser prizes such as the Pulitzer Prize, and the National Book Award, though this has as yet achieved little standing outside the book business. So far as the accouterments of living are concerned the intellectuals tend to play them down; they fill their somewhat ramshackle houses with books, pamphlets and back copies of magazines in living room, library, hall, and cellar. An intellectual cherishes his library with a passion akin to that of the manager of a small industrial plant for his Cadillac.

We don't need to look in any detail at other pyramidal groups or their aristocracies, but I would like to mention a few of the characteristics of some of the others, and to suggest some paradoxes.

Several years ago in an article called "The Social Structure of the Underworld," Lewis Dent, who spent many years in prison, described in *Harper's Magazine* the nature of underworld aristocracy. At the top of the scale are the "heavy thieves," for, as he explains, the thief is regarded as the real professional of the underworld. He is a legitimate criminal, a natural-born enemy of authority (and especially of the police), and he has a sense of community with his own kind that precludes his ever giving any quarter to guards at the expense of his fellows. A proper reform school education contributes to their standing. "At the top are the 'right' guys," Dent wrote, ". . . those who regulate their lives by the distinctive underworld morality. . . . Then come the 'legit' prisoners—average citizens who for one reason or another have run afoul of the law; embezzlers, wife-killers, rapists, and the like. At the bottom of the social scale are the 'wrong' convicts, the creeps—prisoners who violate the code to which they pay lip service." Among these, he says, was a man one might think would have been considered an aristocrat of the underworld, Al Capone. He had no standing in stir because he "was on back-slapping terms with guards and higher officials, slept in silk pajamas on a cot with springs fitted with a real mattress ... and entertained visitors of both sexes privately." Dent believes that the social ostracism that Capone later met in Alcatraz, where the population was "almost 100 per cent elite heavy thieves," led to his final mental collapse.

In the world of big business the corporation is the social microcosm, and its equivalent of Burke's *Peerage* is the *Directory of Directors*. A listing in *Who's Who in America* is a good measure of the eminence of a business executive. (*Who's Who*, incidentally, lists fewer business executives than college professors, but it lists nearly three times as many as authors. Lawyers are almost, though not quite, as numerous as business executives.) The *Social Register* counts for less and less these days except as a convenient local address book and as a "sucker" list. It may still have status implications for the wives of executives, but it is doubtful if executives themselves pay any attention to it. One prominent member of this pyramid, John Hay Whitney, insisted that his name be removed from the New York *Social Register* because he doesn't believe in that sort of social classifying of people. The social structure of the corporation is almost as neatly defined by levels of command as the Army or the Navy; it is a ladder that can be climbed by the intelligent, industrious, and imaginative man if he also has the social graces that are required of his position. His wife, as W. H. Whyte, Jr., has vividly described

2 2 . . .

in *Is Anybody Listening?* must also have the requisite social
gifts if he is to rise to the top. But the tight little aristocracy
of big business is the big men at the top of the biggest corporations—of General Motors and Ford and Chrysler, of
General Electric, Westinghouse, and U.S. Steel.

We are likely to think of their status symbols as luxurious
houses in the older and better established suburbs, country
estates, memberships in half a dozen country clubs, yachts
anchored in Florida waiting for their whim, and company
airplanes at their beck and call. We underestimate them. It is
true that many of them have these luxuries, but it is also
true that they are more likely to be considered the badges
of success by their wives, to whom they leave matters of
taste, than by themselves. The status symbols that they covet
for themselves (and get) are like those of the intellectuals
—honorary degrees. They are posts on the boards of universities and colleges and foundations, and posts in the upper
reaches of government, preferably at the Cabinet or am-
bassadorial levels. It is in this way that the corporation aristocrat achieves not only what he considers equality with the
intellectual aristocracy but some power over the intellectual's world. He becomes the practical man of culture, the
"sound" man behind the "dreamer." Compared with this
status a garage full of Cadillacs and Continentals and a
stable of race horses is nothing.

In actual practice the aristocrat of the business pyramid

stands in some awe of the professional intellectual, regards him with real respect, and woos his approval. He goes to a great deal of trouble, especially in universities, to further the scholar's intellectual pursuits and to guard his freedom. The cases (and they are, of course, the most publicized ones) where businessmen hobble and fetter the faculties over which they have the power of trustees are, I believe, the exceptions and not the rule.

When, however, two aristocracies are in direct competition with each other, this same sweetness does not obtain. There is little communication between the labor aristocracy and the aristocracy of business, except at long range. You do not find James C. Petrillo of the Musicians Union dining with General Sarnoff of the National Broadcasting Company, or Mr. Reuther fishing in Florida with Mr. Ford. The aristocrats of these two pyramids do not even negotiate directly, as neither will—in the best tradition of aristocratic behavior—risk his dignity over a wrangle with the other. They meet through their negotiators, frequently lawyers whose position in the hierarchies of both business and labor is like that of courtiers.

The status symbols of the labor pyramid and the business pyramid are not unlike. Their conventions take place in equally fancy hotels in Florida with equally elaborate entertainments. They travel with equal comfort and in comparable luxury. They eat in the same restaurants, even if

they do not belong to the same clubs. And labor leaders are just as concerned in their way with culture as business leaders are in theirs. It is interesting to note, however, that the language of the labor movement maintains from its history a term that is more class conscious than any used by business. "Rank and file" is a labor term that sets the worker apart from the labor leader as the term "employee" does not set the worker apart from the business leader who is, in actuality, an employee himself.

There is a group whose members occupy rather lordly positions wherever they find themselves and they are likely to find themselves momentarily attached now to one pyramid and now to another. They are the intellectual floaters. They each have a home base, but they serve whatever interests in whichever pyramid their services are required, and they are likely, chameleon-like, to adopt the pattern against which they are set. The lawyers constitute one such group; the architects constitute another. The partners of the prominent law firms (or law factories, as they have been called) while they perform services of all sorts for large and small corporations (and often handle the divorces and other private affairs of their executives) have an identity apart from business. They cannot be said to belong to the intellectual pyramid, though they frequently serve its members and its institutions. Like university economists who act as management consultants they are not big wheels on their own; they are the grease in somebody else's big wheel. Only a few of them, lawyers like Thomas E. Dewey and architects like Wallace K. Harrison, are accepted as equals.

When a scientist leaves a university laboratory to be put in charge, say, of a big manufacturer's missile project, he becomes a VIP in several new leagues at once—political, military, and commercial. And when a practical intellectual like Harlan Cleveland, who was a civil servant and subsequently executive editor of *The Reporter*, becomes a dean at Syracuse, he moves from one pyramid to another by cutting across them near the top level. Of course, these floaters always run the risk of being regarded as foreigners, as "not one of us," by the aristocrats of the several pyramids who have already worked their way up the slopes. The professor who writes speeches for politicians or memos for government committees, for example, may find that he has lost caste in his own bailiwick without ever quite becoming accepted outside it.

There is a good deal of flirtation that goes on between the inhabitants of one pyramid and those of another, and often they try to score points by talking each others' language. "We found," said Meyer Kestnbaum, president of Hart, Schaffner & Marx, of a conference attended by both academics and businessmen, "that our industrialists on the whole were trying to be theoretical and our academic people were trying to be practical." Margaret Mead remarked

of the same conference, held by the Corning Glass Company in 1951, that she had "never seen less signs of people not understanding each other . . . Once in a while somebody remembered that he ought to be misunderstood by the other side, but it took skill to do it." David Riesman has also called attention to this "homogenization" of our society, with corporations cuddling up to colleges, engineers cuddling up to philosophers; Republicans worried about not being loved by eggheads, eggheads worried about not being loved by Republicans; children trying to act like adults, adults trying to "understand" children; women getting more manly and men more womanly. But even if the milk is being whirled and shaken into a uniform product, Americans like cream; and if they can't get it off the top of the bottle they are still going to insist on having it—light, medium, and heavy—in some sort of package.

But while the cream continues to rise to the top the labels on the packages have been changed; the old upper and middle and lower classes have gone out of fashion. There is no place where the Bradley Martins who retired to London would fit into the social scheme which is rapidly replacing the world in which they lived. There is no pyramid for the idle rich; there is only a diminishing fringe for them. They belong neither with the growing number of "retirees" (as they are now called), nor with the occupationally unemployable. They thrived on a class consciousness which they took for granted, but which is now only an illusion.

' If, however, as I suggest, our world is divided vertically instead of horizontally, communication between groups has not and is not likely to break down. It is not maintained by the aristocrats at the top; it is maintained by a social class (and it can only be called that) which cuts across the pyramids and provides an effective means of communication among them. This class, for want of a better term, I call the Upper Bohemians, and they are worth considering more closely and in more detail than any group we have looked at so far.

Chapter III

The Upper Bohemians

THE UPPER BOHEMIANS live in a twilight zone in our society. They are neither below the new aristocracies nor above what we conventionally think of as the middle class. Because they consider themselves to be genuinely unconcerned with the ladder of success, as most Americans see it, they regard the performances and pretensions of the new aristocracies with detached amusement. In recent years they have become a reasonably constant element in a social structure that is not, as we have remarked, notable for its stability. They have dug themselves into the soil of our democracy and, if they will forgive the figure of speech, they perform the useful function, like earthworms, of aerating and fertilizing our topsoil.

A Surfeit of Honey . . . .

We have never had anything quite like them in America before. They are as much at home with the word-men of the communications pyramid as with the vice-president in charge of sales in the business pyramid or the professorial mentors of the intellectuals, though they feel removed from all of them. They are to be found ensconced with labor and, if they are almost never in the forefront of politics, they are frequently in the background, and many of them make their livings in government agencies. Actually they lead a life apart from all of them, and there is a kinship of spirit that makes them stick together as a group—possibly the only cohesive class that we can still put our fingers on.

In Bohemian society it is the convention to look upon all conventions, all codes of behavior, and all rules of taste as matters never to be taken for granted. Conventions by their very nature are regarded with suspicion, for on the surface they seem to have been devised only to obscure and make palatable man's basic inhumanity to man. It is the convention of Bohemianism to say, "To hell with all that; we live by the rules of our own morality."

Traditionally the Bohemian is a romanticist with his eyes raised to the higher truths of art and nature, a walking protest against social sham and all sorts of rules of behavior. He is a man in search of the truth who finds it in the cold north light of a studio garret. There he makes love and

poetry and song and worries about his soul; he does not fret about tomorrow or yesterday or about wealth or position or any of the cushions of life that we now group under the unromantic heading of Security. This is the 'vie de Bohème' or simon-pure kind of Bohemianism of song and story, of the old Left Bank and the old Greenwich Village, of Murger and berets and beards.

It is a far cry from the Upper Bohemianism of today, though some of the romanticism remains, some of the soul-searching, some of the mannerisms of social revolt, or at least of social eccentricity. The Upper Bohemians look down on the new aristocracies, or perhaps they look sideways at them. In either case they couldn't exist without them.

But let me explain, if I can, who they are and what place they occupy in our social galaxy and what their function is. Perhaps I can best do this by introducing you to a few of them at the risk of your already knowing them as well as I do.

Mr. and Mrs. U. B. happen to live in New York, though you might as easily meet them in Cincinnati or Chicago or Los Angeles; you are not apt to find more than a handful of their likes in smaller cities or towns. Their house is a remodeled brownstone, possibly somewhat modernized on the outside but still largely indistinguishable from the other houses in the block. If you were to peer through the living-

room window, you would notice that they indulge in rather
definite and slightly odd colors on the walls, have rather
more than the usual number of books, some drawings and
probably a painting or two—one an abstraction and one a
somewhat unconventional landscape—and possibly a mobile.
Their house is not in a currently fashionable part of town;
it is not close to Park Avenue, for instance; but neither is it
in an unfashionable district, nor a socially improper one.
They live, one might say, not quite on the fringe but, rather,
on the verge. The twilight of residence between the fashionable and the worthy is their natural habitat out of convic-
tion. They do not want to be classified.

Mr. U. B. is a publisher, though he might as easily be a
lawyer, or a writer, or an architect, or an editor, or, but
somewhat less likely, a member of a business managerial
team. If he is in business, the chances are that he is in some
aspect of it that deals with words—in advertising or public
relations or some other form of "communications" that grat-
ifies his sense of being involved with interpretation. There
are, however, some Upper Bohemians who are "strictly
business" in any big corporation, free spirits who are models
of buttoned-down-collar conformity on the job but quite
independent of their business associates and deportment
after five o'clock. They move, as I have suggested, from
whatever pyramid gives them a living into the company of
other Upper Bohemians from other pyramids. Since Upper

Bohemians are given to the discussion and exploration of large ideas set in a social context, they provide an open and continuously flowing channel of communication between pyramids. They discuss their business problems, not as most businessmen discuss them in "how's business?" terms or in specific techniques of marketing or their troubles with labor, but abstractly as social problems. They are concerned not with nuts and bolts but with the relationships of the corporation to the community, not with supply and demand but with ebb and flow.

In his professional or in his extracurricular life Mr. U. B. often moves in and out of the arts or near them, but in any case he calls them by their pet names and is alive to their latest alarums and excursions. He is aware of what exhibitions are on Fifty-seventh Street, what plays are current and imminent, and he has definite convictions about which ones he will bother to see and which he will eschew. The same might be said of his attitude toward current books, motion pictures, and ballet. He is culturally hep, but he is not a cultural hepcat. Many things interest him but few things "send" him. He is a sophisticated patron of the arts, so sophisticated that for the most part he lets other people gamble on them. His discriminating taste in paintings and books and furniture has nothing, he is convinced, to do with fashion; it has only to do with permanent quality. He is not likely to be a collector in any orderly or elaborate way;

that sort of thing he leaves to the aristocrats who collect under the guidance of a dealer and who have, he believes, no taste of their own. He is merely an acquirer of miscellaneous items of artistic or literary interest. For this reason his house is customarily furnished with a chef's salad of a few modern pieces and a good many old, "amusing" ones—nineteenth-century Gothic, for example—and just plain comfortable and unclassifiable and well-made upholstered pieces that by no standards of taste are "objectionable." Mr. U. B. wouldn't be caught dead reading *House and Garden* or *House Beautiful.* He is not in the least worried about his taste or concerned with being told what is chic. He might, on the other hand, subscribe to an architectural magazine because he is interested in changes in style. He makes a sharp distinction between fashion and style. Anyone can follow fashion, he believes; only a man of taste can distinguish style.

His wife, Mrs. U. B., shares this attitude, as is evidenced most clearly by her manner of dress. She isn't above peeking into *Vogue* or *Harper's Bazaar* though it is usually to complain about what she finds there. She dresses in her own style, which is likely to be a slightly eccentric version of what other women are wearing and may even be a "thing" she has picked off the rack at Klein's or Ohrbach's and endowed with her own touch. Her costume jewelry is "Victorian heirloom" or extravagantly fake in order that it may

make no pretense of looking like real jewelry. Ideally she would like a piece of brass cut into a mobile by Alexander Calder, big and bold and defiant, but short of that a chunk of Mexican silver or even small jadeite rocks or something that looks like an old bedspring will suffice. But whatever it may be, it is not a cheap copy of something expensive. Expensive conventional jewels, like expensive furs, are, she believes, a mere matter of publishing one's bank balance on one's person. That is for the socially pretentious or the socially insecure, not for her. Furthermore she discards garments that merely have what she derisively calls a "well-bred" or a "ladies' club" look. She owns a hat ("In case I need it for a funeral or something . . ."), but never wears it if she can help it, which she usually can.

Her husband's dress is not eccentric, but it is casual. The tweed jacket and slacks as a costume for office wear were almost surely introduced not by sportsmen, who are strong adherents to the conventional costume for the proper occasion, but by Upper Bohemians, who put comfort and casualness before routine propriety. The Upper Bohemian would not, however, wear the loud be-palmed and be-flowered sports shirt with its abbreviated tails hanging outside his slacks; his country play clothes are more likely than not to be the true countryman's work clothes. Not long ago I saw ✗ on a railroad platform in rural Connecticut what I consider the quintessence of Upper Bohemian male attire—

army shoes, a red-and-black woolen shirt, and dungarees. From the wearer's watch pocket hung a Victorian gold chain dangling a Phi Beta Kappa key.

From their outward appearance you will see that Mr. and Mrs. U. B. are more confident and more free-and-easy about their taste than are the members of the various aristocracies who depend on decorators to give consistency and style to their homes (or rely on accepted conventions) and couturiers to embellish their persons. But how do they live? What goes on in these somewhat eccentric houses and in these unconventional clothes?

Let us look first at some of the more superficial aspects of Upper Bohemian life before we attempt to see what lies beneath the casual surface. The surface, first of all, is casual; life in the Upper Bohemian household is studiedly informal. It might almost be said that an Upper Bohemian will always sit on the floor in preference to a chair in any room where a group is gathered, no matter how many chairs there may be. He also prefers his dinner on a card table in the living room to sitting at a dining-room table conventionally accoutered. His attitude toward servants (though he would be unlikely to refer to anyone as a servant, lest the word sound patronizing) is cozy rather than pretentious. He doesn't care a fig about maids in black dresses and white aprons; that is merely sham for sham's sake. He would always rather have a rough-

and-ready type who is "an instinctive cook" than a trained maid who understands the art of waiting on table. He wants his meals when he wants them, and he has a special intolerance of anyone whose life is dictated by what he calls "a tyranny of servants." In his mind the only justification for service is to make life more relaxed, not more formal, though if he happens to be well off (which he not infrequently is) his parties may be well staffed and rather quietly elegant.

This relaxed attitude toward convention is typical of the Upper Bohemian and basic in the pattern of his behavior. But there is in his mind always a good reason for unconventionality, for he is not sloppy in his manners. He merely thinks of manners of all sorts as an expression of good will, not of good training. He treats his friends in a somewhat offhand and casual way which he expects them to accept as a sign of affection. He assumes that they are perceptive of his moods and do not need to be treated like strangers or children; they should know that if he disliked them he would be elaborately polite to them. Only rarely, only when provoked, and only to a member of one of the aristocracies would he be elaborately rude.

If he is a true Upper Bohemian and a serious one, he scarcely dares to let down the bars that separate him from the conservatism of the new aristocracies or from what he would call the "middle-class moralities." His horror of the philistinism of Main Street is exceeded only by his amusement at the cultural pretensions of Park Avenue and Beverly Hills and Westchester. He looks upon all culture but his own, all other standards of behavior, and all other measures of success with tolerant suspicion.

✗   If other people are likely to underestimate the importance of the Upper Bohemians, the Upper Bohemians are likely to overestimate themselves. Their number is not legion, and yet there are more of them than one might suspect from a superficial look at one's own community or one's friends. I have suggested that they are most likely to be found in fairly sizable and large cities, but you will find them also wherever there is an academic community, such as, for example, Princeton, New Jersey, which is within difficult but possible commuting distance of a metropolis. Some of the Upper Bohemians in such a community are directly connected with the university, but many others have moved there because they like the pleasant breeze of intellectualism that blows off such an academic reservoir. They enjoy the opportunity to number among their friends those whose profession requires them to think in large and abstract terms about the arts or about the state of the world, and they like to mingle with others who put, often perforce, the satisfactions of the mind and spirit ahead of those of social status. While there is social status within a university (indeed,

there may be no other society save the Army so rigidly classified), the scholar is to the world outside the university a classless man, and so the Upper Bohemians find him congenial.

You are unlikely to find the Upper Bohemian in the suburbs which closely surround big cities; if he is a suburbanite (a name he would abhor) he lives in the more inaccessible and peripheral suburbs, so that he and his wife can enjoy the freedom of the country without fear of being observed over the back fence by neighbors. They want to sunbathe stark naked if they feel like it. You will not, however, find them in a remote surburb in which there are no others of their own kind. Upper Bohemians are no less gregarious than most people, though they are strong in their protestations of independence and confident of their ability to keep themselves entertained.

They are not joiners and are likely to shun country clubs, ladies' clubs, civic organizations, and all other forms of what they consider artificially contrived social media. It doesn't occur to them that the fact that they run in droves, that any party they may go to is likely to consist of the same dozen or so couples making the same kinds of conversation (art, politics, music, books) over the same kinds of drinks (martinis, bourbon, wine and soda) is very like the country-club pattern without the country club.

Wherever an Upper Bohemian may travel in this country

or abroad he will, if he sticks to the sizable cities, always land with his own kind. There is a sort of unacknowledged and unofficial grapevine by which he travels, and if he goes from New York to Denver or San Francisco, for instance, he finds himself with letters of introduction to a business-man-poet or a physician who paints, and he will soon be taken to the bosom of the local Upper Bohemia. Further-more he will discover that nearly everyone he meets knows a friend of his or a friend of a friend. This same grapevine will lead him to his own kind in London, Paris, and Rome; he can go anywhere without ever leaving Upper Bohemia more than a day's journey ahead or behind.

The Upper Bohemian might be willing to concede that he is something of an intellectual snob. He does, after all, set more store by intellectual pursuits than does any other group except the professional academics and the artists. If he lives geographically in a sort of social no man's land, he also lives in a sort of intellectual neutral zone. He thinks of himself as a bridge between the bright light of intellectual-ism and the artificially illuminated world of affairs. His con-versation bears this out. Unlike most people's conversation which proceeds from the general to the specific, from "How's business?" to the price of gaskets, his is apt to go from the specific to the general. A casual remark about a tomato is likely to end in a heated discussion of the com-parative values of organic gardening, or a reference to a

Buick to a speculative argument about the state of American industrial design. The Upper Bohemian likes to see things in the large and to savor their implications.

The same might be said of his attitude toward his children. Children are problems before they are people, and as a parent he is full of theories about the rounded development of the complete personality. For this reason he inclines toward progressive schools and away from traditional institutions.

He encourages his children to call him and his wife and their friends by their first names, and to engage in adult conversations which as often as not mystify and benumb them. This is part and parcel of his theory that every child is a little adult whose mind should be stretched and whose interests should parallel his parents'. This forced growth and overinsistence on intellectual interests in some cases breeds hardened little philistines and in other cases monstrous little prodigies; it also breeds its fair share of average children.

The Upper Bohemian attitude toward sex may be summarized as open-minded. He is not a defender of promiscuity, but he maintains such a tolerant attitude toward other people's behavior that he often finds it exceedingly difficult to make clear-cut decisions for himself. When an Upper Bohemian talks about his doctor, it is a safe guess that he is as likely to be talking about his psychiatrist as about his physician, but his readiness to seek psychiatric advice is probably sound. Because the Upper Bohemians recognize the uses of psychiatry, I doubt very much if the incidence of mental breakdown among them is as high as it is among the aristocracies or the middle classes, who think of psychiatrists as witch doctors.

There may, however, be a quite different reason for this stability. The Upper Bohemian is essentially secure in his social position. He is more likely to be interested in keeping even with "the people" than up with the Joneses.

To understand this we must retrace our steps for a moment and consider the origins of the Upper Bohemian. What is it that endows him with this sense of security that makes it possible for him to stand apart and look at other strata of society, to consider their mores, and to fashion a style of living and a code of belief out of his distrust for theirs? Let's see where he came from and how he has got where he is.

The Upper Bohemians do not lend themselves to statistical analysis, but they come mainly from two socially secure segments of society. It would be my guess that the largest number are the sons and daughters of the professional classes, the offspring of the law and medicine, of academics and clergymen. They have been brought up in an atmosphere in which the achievements of the mind have been put ahead of

the achievements of the bank balance—if not actually, then at least conversationally and by precept. It is well, in this connection, to remember that there is always in the back of the mind of the professional man the comforting thought that if he is not a financial success he can without losing face be an "interesting intellectual"; no one holds it against an intellectual that he hasn't made money; on the contrary, it is unfashionable for him to do so. When, however, a professional man makes a great deal of money, as writers and architects occasionally do and lawyers do far more often, he is likely to regard this bonanza as something over and beyond his real satisfactions in life and not essential to them. In this respect he is obviously quite distinct from the businessman who, when he has accumulated his wealth, then looks around at the cultural ornaments of life and decides in which ones he would like to indulge.

So it is out of professional families that I believe the largest number of today's Upper Bohemians have come. They have been brought up to mistrust the kind of life in which money and the ostentation that it can buy are all-important. During the past ten or fifteen years the status of the intellectual in America has risen considerably in the social scale as we noted in the last chapter. Today's progeny of yesterday's intellectuals have a newly built-in social position. In order to maintain this status and not let it become confused with other and to them less distinguished social groups they have formed their own—though they would be the last ones to recognize how neatly stratified they have become.

Also into the Upper Bohemian group have migrated the intellectually inclined sons and daughters of the rich who are embarrassed about Father's lack of what they would call "any real culture." They come from a socially secure group well versed in the gentle amenities of decorous behavior and well able to give their children all of what are known as "the advantages." These scions of wealth and manners are refugees to Upper Bohemia, seeking sanctuary from aristocratic stuffiness.

The third main reservoir of recruits for Upper Bohemia is more difficult to define because it has no single character and no clear edges. It might be called the Pool of the Arts, for it is fed by streams from all the social classes. Into it flows a steady trickle of moderately to considerably successful, intellectually respectable, and socially perceptive writers, artists, academics, and architects, along with a few actors. Many of them are "bright young things," extremely clever, extremely ambitious, and already at a tender age self-made. Acceptability in Upper Bohemian circles is to them the achievement of a social ambition. To them Upper Bohemia is a desirable sort of aristocracy to which to belong, and of all the Upper Bohemians they are the most conscientiously and cautiously Bohemian.

It cannot be denied that the Upper Bohemian serves a useful purpose in our cultural and civic life. Since he believes that his interests are not identified with those of any special social or economic class he serves as a minor social, political, and cultural balance wheel. He is a believer in social progress but, as he is not a faddist, he is suspicious and scornful of dogma; sometimes his beliefs and his suspicions cancel each other out and leave him inert. This is not to say, however, that he is a middle-of-the-roader; he is far more likely to be on one side of the road on some questions and on the other side on others. In general, however, you will find that the Upper Bohemian inclines to take the side of the labor aristocracy against the business aristocracy, inclines to the Freudian interpretation of behavior, and the Keynesian interpretation of economics, and a free-thought interpretation of religion. He goes overboard about none of these. His deepest belief is in personal and intellectual freedom. He is not a theorist, though he enjoys theory, any more than he is a realist (as the businessman uses that word) though he is a respecter of the realities.

Where the arts are concerned he keeps what he dearly hopes is an open mind. He believes in freedom of expression and he resents the recent political incursions into arguments about the arts. He will argue violently on one side or the other of such a question as whether the main current in painting today is abstractionist, but the question is of far less moment to him than whether or not there seems to be vitality in the arts in general. He deplores the commercialism of television, and settles this problem for himself either by not having a set or by using one with fastidious discrimination. He considers the movies an art form, and his attitude toward them, as toward other arts, stresses the honest, as he calls it, against the pretentious.

Not all of his behavior in relation either to the arts or to the world around him is aloof. He likes to mix with other kinds of people, to take part in causes in which he believes, even to do menial jobs in a political campaign (part of his pride is in making it quite clear that he doesn't think he is better than other people—just different), so long as he can escape into his own comfortable Bohemianism when he is through with his job. He does not really want to be one of the boys any more than Lady Bountiful wants to be one of the girls, but while he is with them he wants to be identified as one with the people though not quite one of them.

One of the characteristics of traditional Bohemianism has always been its questionable respectability in the eyes of the community. It has been looked on by all classes of society as something not quite real—by the poor as an affectation of poverty by people who could be better off if they wanted to be, by the middle classes as darn fools and dreamers who

are free and easy in their morals and have no fear of God or the Treasury Department, and by the upper classes as quaint. But the real strength of the Bohemians and their vital function, both of which are out of all proportion to their numbers, has been rooted in their eagerness to flout convention for the purpose, sometimes sincere and sometimes affected, of fostering new ideas and bringing about the destruction of sham and flummery.

In this the Upper Bohemian believes, and if he is caught in a kind of sham and flummery that is all his own, he is not aware of it. If he were aware of it, it is unlikely that it would bother him, because, remember, he is not only a social introvert but an observer and in some ways a self-appointed policeman of the social scene. He is not above casting a critical eye upon himself, though when he does he is inclined to be pleased with what he sees. His tribe, I believe, is somewhat on the increase in spite of what seems to many to be a tendency toward conformity and standardization of taste and behavior. It may well be that it is because the tide runs strong in that direction that a respectable kind of Bohemianism has such a strong appeal to so many who do not want to be caught by conformity but who are not willing to risk the opprobrium of being radicals.

There is always a reservoir of eager spirits who wish to enjoy the titivation of flouting convention, and yet do not want to stray far from the warmth of a secure social hearth. There are always those who believe that they can take convention or leave it. Those who leave it with a flourish are true Bohemians. It is those who manage to take it *and* leave it who are the true Upper Bohemians.

Chapter IV

The New Servant Class

ALL SOCIAL classes, even the Upper Bohemians, are divided down the middle by a line which, however classless we may think we are, maintains a state of social tension. On one side of the line are men; on the other women. Only children, who are more or less sexless up to the point where they begin to think of little else, straddle the line and spread their favors and disfavors with equal grace, behaving, regardless of their sex, now like little boys and now like little girls. Women, in their battle for equality with men, have been scrubbing for a long time the line that divides adults, and they occasionally create the illusion that it doesn't exist any more. It is only an illusion, but sometimes in our day it seems appallingly close to a reality.

Look what has happened to the innocent, peace-loving husband in this best of all possible worlds.

Recently a friend of mine told me of a telephone conversation he had had with a young man who is a neighbor of his.

"I wish I could," the young man said. "There's nothing I'd like better, but I'm up to my elbows in diapers." The young neighbor is the father of two, the more recent one very recent indeed. My friend had asked him to play tennis, and he reported to me that, when he hung up, his feeling was not one of surprise or pity; it was one of guilt.

"I didn't say to myself, 'The poor hen-pecked fellow'," he told me with some shock in his voice. "I just said to myself, 'Well, I guess I ought to be doing my household chores too.' What kind of reaction do you call that?"

The narrow-gauge train of thought that this conversation set in motion in my mind led me to speculate about the nature of husbands and the recent changes in their behavior around the house. How did it happen that my friend's friend was diapering and that my friend thought he should be dusting or waxing? What would my father have thought of such behavior? I laughed out loud.

Bernard DeVoto once remarked to a colleague of mine, "What every career woman needs is a good wife." When he made this observation a number of years ago, the atmosphere of marriage was somewhat different from the

atmosphere today. Only a woman with a career was then expected to have someone else assume the burdens of the household for her. It is only quite recently that (in cities and suburbs especially) every woman, regardless of her notions about a career, has adopted a different attitude. Now she takes it for granted that, when she marries, she is bound to get, almost as though it were a package deal, a husband who is also a part-time wife.

To call him a wife is, perhaps, to put it too bluntly. He is rather more servant than wife, though the distinction is sometimes a fine one. With a few interesting exceptions, the roles of the husband and wife are becoming less and less sharply differentiated. Whereas it was once a question of "Who wears the pants in this family?" it is now a matter of pants all around, and the children are as likely to cling to Father's apron strings as Mother's. You may have noticed that, in recent years, women have come to refer to their husbands more and more often as their "mates"—a sexually indeterminate word and one that implies equality. Man, once known as "the head of the family," is now partner in the family firm, part-time man, part-time mother and part-time maid. He is the chief cook and bottle washer; the chauffeur, the gardener, and the houseboy; the maid, the laundress, and the charwoman.

If you are in any doubt that this is so, let me produce for you what are known as "the findings" of our favorite oracles, the pollsters. Crosley says that more than a third of the husbands in several of our northeastern states do the dishes, clean house and look after the children, and more than half of them do a lot of the shopping. The Gallup poll insists that 62 per cent of American husbands are intimate with dishwater and about 40 per cent help with the cooking. Kenneth Fink, director of the Princeton Research Service, has discovered that, in New York, 87 per cent of the young men from twenty-one to twenty-nine help with the housework, but there seems to be some slight advantage in growing older. Only 70 per cent of men over forty-five are part-time women. This suggests that patience and geriatrics may ultimately lick the husband's domestic problem, but he shouldn't count on it.

How did women get into this frame of mind and men into this fix? What has happened to the shape and texture of family life in America? What has become of the servants of another day? What are men turning into with their aprons and safety pins and dishpan hands? If it is anybody's fault, whose fault is it? What drives this creature, the man who is part-time wife, and what keeps him in order? It is a puzzling lot of questions, but let's look.

The pollsters' findings suggest the first of our questions: How did men get in this fix? And that question cannot be answered without looking at how the position of women

has changed and without finding out what has become of yesterday's servants.

It is doubtful that when men let women have the vote, back in 1920, they foresaw the sort of social revolution that they were letting loose on themselves. It is unlikely that they caught the slightest glimmer of a future in which they would share not only the political decisions of the nation with women, but also the dishpan and the oven and the mop. Actually, the revolution started long before the nineteenth amendment was adopted; it goes back to the time before the turn of the century when men discovered that they would rather have women run the typewriters in offices than run them themselves, and the business career woman, as we know her today, first got a finger hold in man's world. Imperceptibly at first, the distinctions between man's world and woman's world began to blur. Men stopped giving their seats to women on buses and subways and taking off their hats when women entered elevators. "If they are going to compete in our world," men reasoned, "then they should be treated as men."

From the man's point of view, this was a major tactical blunder. He ought to have realized that he should preserve at all costs such distinctions as remained between men and women, and he should have kept the line clean as to what was expected of each. But once he had allowed the social differences of the sexes to be played down, it is only logical that he should ultimately have found himself assuming some of the functions of women. In this sense, the man in the apron has no one to blame but himself.

But it would be unfair to give the impression that the amount of housework performed by men is entirely the result of connivance by women or of their attempt to invade man's world. The gradual shrinking of the old servant class explains part of what has happened. Our changing idea of what constitutes personal success explains another part, as does the shift in our notions about what makes the ideal family. What has happened is partly an economic phenomenon, partly an industrial and mechanical one and partly a social one.

The recent story of the servant class in America might be called "The Transformation of Bridget; or Who Stole the Upstairs Maid from Mrs. Cabot's Mansion?" Bridgets and Maggies and Hildas by the hundreds of thousands arrived in America from many parts of Europe in the sixty years that followed the Civil War. Domestic service was the best employment they could find, and it was also the quickest way for them to learn the customs and manners of the new country. Households with six or seven Bridgets, and their male counterparts, were not uncommon before World War I, and the "servant class" was a rigidly stratified society

(within a much more fluid one) where everyone was supposed to "know his place."

It was World War I that took the duster out of Bridget's hand and replaced it with a wrench. War factories were hungry for workers, and they offered better wages and shorter hours than housewives could afford to give. After the war, in the frantic twenties, some of the Bridgets went back to their old jobs; and in the depression years of the thirties, families that could afford servants found them in plentiful supply. It was war again in 1941 that emancipated the cooks and maids and butlers, and ever since that time, the number of women in domestic service has steadily dwindled. Before World War I, more women worked at domestic service than at any other kind of job; now, with more women employed than ever before in what we like to call peacetime, domestic service ranks fifth.

Something had to fill the undusted and unwashed gap between the career woman and her home. As more and more married women took full-time and part-time jobs, more and more mechanical gadgets were invented to lighten the burdens of housework. Someone, however, had to help run the gadgets for the nine and a quarter million married women who worked. And now we begin to see the answer to the question of how men got themselves into their present domestic fix.

Henry Dreyfuss, the industrial designer, has called American women "gadget-conscious mammals." But it is well known that if you want to get an American male to do manual labor, he is a sucker for anything that whirs or hums or lights up. He is wafted aloft like the pilot of a jet; he becomes "the man at the controls," a Walter Mitty. He identifies himself far more easily with the flying saucer than with the saucer in the sink, and women know this.

With the war over and servants increasingly hard to come by, especially at prices that middle-class families could afford, washing machines, dishwashers, freezers, electric floor waxers and a multiplicity of other devices from mixers to mangles flooded the gadget shops (called appliance stores) which suddenly appeared on main streets of towns everywhere. Men, with their supposed superior knowledge of mechanical things, were consulted for the first time on the purchase of expensive pieces of domestic equipment, and before you could say "Change the water after each using," they were running them. As domestically unskilled labor, husbands came to pride themselves on being able to operate machines which manufacturers had so designed that they practically ran themselves.

But the scarcity of servants and the flood of gadgets that could be bought on time payments tell only part of the story of man's new captivity by women. World War II tore many families apart, and when they were put back

With nobody to cook and serve dinner at a given hour, we eat when we please and where we please—in the living room, in the back yard, in the kitchen. Not so long ago, most families, whether they could afford servants or not, used to observe many of the same formalities observed in families who were elaborately waited on. Now the families who can still afford servants affect many of the informalities of those who have none. The tables, you might say, have been turned into trays on the lap, the sit-down dinner has become a feast of squat-and-scramble. Some member of the family is always on his feet fetching something from the kitchen. Families, like toasters, have become pop-up, and Father no longer sits and is waited on.

My friend's neighbor who couldn't play tennis because of the diapers is the servant-father in just such a family, and so, according to the poll takers, are a majority of the other husbands in America.

Briefly, then, this is how men have got themselves into what is not only a new role but a new frame of mind, and this brings us abruptly to the question: what sort of man is this member of the new servant class? How does he think of himself and what keeps him going? It will take him a long time to fight his way out of the cage that he has helped to build for himself. It has been men, we must remember, who have invented, promoted and sold the mechanical

we are expressing our freedom from the bigness and imper-
sonality of the world in which we earn our living and in
which most of us are cogs and few of us are wheels. But this
is a large generality about a large motive. What does it mean
in the communities in which we live?

It has come to pass that a man sharing the jobs of the
household with his wife is an increasingly accepted part of
the pattern of American family life. Indeed, in many communities, a man who doesn't help with the dishes and the
dusting and the beds is regarded as only half a man. He is
considered lazy or overbearing, or he is thought not to love
his wife and children. Furthermore, he is selfish and he is
failing to "fulfill" himself, and these epithets are not applied
to him just by women but by other men in the community
as well. Probably, however, none of them accurately describes him. It would be nearer the truth to say that he is
out of date, living in a world that is gone and is not likely
to return. He is the vestigial remnant of another age in
which a man's position in the community was measured by
the number of people who contributed to his creature com-
forts rather than by what he contributed to the community.

Whether we like it or not (and we apparently like it or
we wouldn't put up with it on such a scale), the new pattern of life with the husband as a working member of the
cast rather than as a spoiled financial backer has become the

together again, a strange new domestic pattern emerged that was quite unlike anything Americans had ever seen before. Millions of veterans went to college or to professional or trade schools on the GI bill. Many of these men were married and had small children, and in order to make ends meet, young wives went out and got jobs. Father, who had learned to make beds, darn socks, and police up in the Army, was left with his books and his babies and his broom. He became not only a wife but a mother, and he was grateful for the chance to re-establish his life in this way, hopeful that the day would come when he might take off his apron and get out in the world. Those were the days when men used to gather in the self-service laundry and swap stories as they once had in the corner bar.

With our usual adaptability we have taken the shortage of servants, the influx of gadgets, the domestic skills that men learned as soldiers, the new role of women and docility of men, and out of them have created a new mode of life. Our image of the ideal family has changed from one in which Father laid down the law while Mother made the wheels go round to something far more like a team roughly the size and character of a basketball team. The ball is passed from hand to hand and the responsibility is shared by everybody.

At the same time, we have become devoted to what Frederick Lewis Allen called "the cult of informality."

gadgets that now enslave them, though they did it in the name of making the little woman's burden lighter. Also, it is men who have fought for the shorter work week so that they might, as it has turned out, have longer weekends to clean out the cellar and paint the shutters and more hours in the evening to help with the dishes. They have made their own beds, and now they must lie in them. Futhermore, the chances are that they must get up in the morning and make them again.

It is too soon to divide husbands into neat categories within the new servant class. They are a higgledy-piggledy lot, self-assertive at the same time that many of them (but by no means all) are docile. There are those who complain bitterly that they have lost their freedom; there are as many others who take the new shape of the family for granted. But before housemaid's knee gets to be known as husband's knee, let us examine some of the motives that make the members of the new servant class behave as they do. Some of these motives lie deep in the natures of men; others have to do with the nature of the times we live in.

In the first place, we must consider the part that vanity, as strong and timeless a motive as any, plays in the behavior of the husband-servant. It is no secret to women that female vanity is usually a means to an end, but that male vanity is an end in itself. It is also no secret that male vanity is easily played upon by sensible and clever women, even the nicest of women, and that its proper manipulation is the most reliable means of converting a husband into an adequate servant. There are two main techniques for applying the alchemy that turns the leaden mate into the golden slave. One is challenge and the other is flattery.

More often than not, the man with the hammer in his hand or with the waxer whirring at his feet is so employed because his wife has either suggested that he might not be clever enough to do the job, or because she has implied that nobody could do it as well as he. ("Darling," she says, "I suppose it's too big a job for you, but . . ." or "Would you mind? Nobody can make it glisten the way you can.") In either case, something more than just family responsibility has spurred his efforts. It is vanity as surely as it is muscle that drives the nail or brings the floor to a gleam. But vanity goes further than merely sweetening the occasional chore; it plays its part in the performance of the routine job as well.

It is difficult to isolate vanity from any of the other deep-seated motives that cause men to assume their new share of household chores, for it runs through their performance of most of them. But we must make a distinction here between those chores that are traditionally the jobs of servants and those which have been regarded as what a man was expected "to do around the house."

Maintenance has, to a very great extent, always been Father's job. When he could afford not to do it himself, he ordered it done, but, in either case, it came within his domain and not his wife's. So it is in the maintenance jobs that the man feels at home with himself, for it is easier for him to picture himself with a hammer in his hand than with a dustpan and brush. He is happier when called upon to repair the screens or fix a drawer that sticks than he is when he is expected to make a bed. He likes those jobs that not only are traditionally man's work but also have a certain permanence about them. Beds never stay made nor dishes clean, but a new screen in the front door is good for years and a man can point to such a job with a pride of accomplishment.

"Do it yourself," in spite of all the smashed thumbs and broken limbs it causes, is a byword of our day, and it is a slogan that applies to more than just maintenance and building—to fixing a faucet or adding a room on the house —it describes a frame of mind that typifies the new husband better than anything else. Doing it ourselves is our answer to more than just the high cost of labor; it is our reply to the machine which has assumed so many of the functions that we have always considered to be our own. We are reclaiming in our small ways what technology has taken away from us in big ways. In performing our small chores, whether they are maintenance jobs or even servants' jobs,

commonly accepted standard of urban and suburban life. We have allowed this aspect of our social revolution to take place, not because of outside pressures on us but because we wanted it to. In a country with as vast wealth as ours, we could, if that were what we wanted, have maintained a traditional servant class, but that did not suit us. We wanted everybody to have as much spiritual elbow room and as much chance to determine his own way of life as possible.

If not many people wanted to go on being servants, that was all right with most of the rest of us; we just moved over a little and took on some of their work while, quite literally, they took on some of ours. They moved into our corner of the labor market, and so we had to take on the chores that they used to perform for us. And we saw to it that we had time to do them. We cut down on our work week at the office and the factory, and we set about to produce the gadgets that would make being our own servants as painless as possible.

But, further than that, we have made a game out of our new system. We have taken to the informal life, the life without the old and often suffocating airs and graces of formality, and moved it out of doors where it has become a picnic, or into the living room where it has become a party. We have divided up the chores so that every member of the family does his share, and the work is disposed of in concert. Mother is no longer the lonely slave in her kitchen or, as some pampered women used to say, a slave to her servants. She is now, at worst, a slave among slaves. Her sentence has been commuted from labor in solitary confinement to light housework, with the children gaily demolishing dishes at her elbow and her husband singing glees to the accompaniment of the humming refuse grinder.

If you are in any doubt that husbands as a servant class are here to stay, let me point out to you a familiar but significant phenomenon. There are still a good many men in America, some of them members of the aristocracies, who can well afford to have servants and do, indeed, have staffs of them. But these same men like to play at being servants themselves in much the same spirit that Marie Antoinette played at milkmaid at the Petit Trianon before the French Revolution. On their penthouse terraces or beside their swimming pools, they preside over a barbecue in chef's cap and apron, clutching long forks in asbestos-gloved hands. They are, in their quaint and self-conscious way, imitating the men who take their household chores as a matter of course.

They are trying to be in the swim, for it has not only become necessary but it seems also to have become chic for husbands not only to stand and wait but also to serve.

Chapter V

The Mass-Produced
Eccentrics

THERE has, moreover, been a genuine revolution in men's clothes since World War II. Whatever the members of the new servant class may have had to concede to women in terms of drudgery they have usurped what has for a long time been considered a right of women—the right to look as pretty as possible. Pretty is an adjective that makes men squirm when it is applied to their appearance, though they will accept it when it refers to any single item of haberdashery such as a tie or a scarf or even a shirt. But men have gone beyond the individual item of prettiness and increasingly they have been dolling themselves up in ensembles—

beach jackets of fancily printed cotton with trunks to match, madras sports jackets with linen slacks in pastel colors, scarlet tuxedo and honey-colored trousers, and the like—which, let them take it or leave it, are meant to be pretty. Whether this is part of the feminization of men, as some psychiatrists have called it, or whether this is just men reverting to a natural instinct to dress up in fancy plumage, it is characteristic of this moment in our history.

Both the personality of a man and his position in life have something to do with the way he gets himself up, but it is possible in these days of "homogenization" for the personality of a man to play a more important part in how he dresses than it used to. The outlandish was once left to eccentrics and Bohemians, and the working classes dressed like the working classes and gentlemen like gentlemen—in some degree. It has always been true in America, or at least it has been true for more than a century, that at a distance it has been nearly impossible to tell the "maid from the mistress," to use a phrase from the first issue of *Harper's Bazaar* in 1867. It has been easier to tell men apart. In some respects it is now easier than ever, and it is to these respects that I would like to direct your attention.

But before I attempt to provide rules of thumb for telling men apart by the cut of their clothes, let us look at what has generally happened to the outer man.

Most obviously he has become more casual. He has taken

66 . . .

to wearing "separates," to use a term from the vocabulary of women's fashions. American men now buy about sixty-two million pairs of slacks a year, which is five times as many as they bought fifteen years ago. To wear with these slacks they buy eight million sports jackets, more than ten times as many as they did in 1940. If this is insufficient evidence of casualness, let me add that sports shirts now outsell regular shirts by 60 per cent. One would think from this that American men did nothing but hang around country clubs.

It is true, of course, that they do hang around more. They have a great deal more time off from their jobs than they used to—shorter working days and longer weekends. But that is only part of the story. Men who would not have thought of appearing at the office in anything but a suit now wear their separates to work, a trend which, as I have mentioned, was probably started by the Upper Bohemians. The nationwide move to the suburbs has unquestionably had a great deal to do with informality in men's dress; millions of men have become country squires, a few on a large scale and many on a small scale. Country squires since the eighteenth century have been wearing jackets that didn't match their trousers, and if the trend continues we may even see the re-emergence of pants which like plus-fours or knickerbockers button just below the knee. The Bermuda-length shorts and long socks which have been struggling for acceptance among men for the past five or six years (and which have been accepted in colleges, in some suburbs, and in resorts, but are still frowned on by Brooks Brothers and garrulous taxi drivers in cities) may be this generation's way of getting grownups into short pants. No self-respecting boy, on the other hand, will be seen in anything but long pants from the age of five on.

Along with the move to the suburbs there are several other changes in our mores which have encouraged the increasing casualness in men's clothes. One is the inevitable do-it-yourself craze, which I have mentioned before, and another is the clamor to be out of doors. The out-of-doors movement has been imposed on the rest of the country by the inhabitants of the Western states, most noticeably California, which is populated by a species of primitive sun worshipers. If you have any doubt of the influence of the West on the East, you need only look at the clothes men wear when doing it themselves.

Do-it-yourself is the biggest thing ever to hit the blue-jeans industry. Manufacturers of work clothes have a brand-new market among what used to be called the white-collar class for pants named "Steadies," "Slimerees," and "Taper Twills," and for work shirts, denim jackets, and work shoes. The phenomenal sale of men's blue jeans is a rare instance of a fad that was first taken up in the East by cowboy-minded teenagers and became a general fashion for their elders, both male and female.

The eagerness with which the suburban male approaches the out-of-doors not only impels him into the garden in work clothes; it also makes him want to eat his barbecued spareribs in the back yard dressed like a bird of paradise. For some reason food seems to taste better to him if he has on blue canvas shoes, brick-red or canary-yellow slacks, and a pastel sports shirt which hangs free, like a young matron's maternity smock, outside the pants. These are symbols of leisure and the good life as advertised by Hollywood. They are also symbols of the revolt against the conformity that is imposed on men by the daily routine of business. Here, supposedly, the free-wheeling spirit is given wings. The country squire becomes the Oriental potentate in fine raiment, and the effect is as quaint as the peasant costumes of any nation.

In the last two decades, as we noted in the last chapter, there has been a continual, though gradual, move in the direction of what seems at first glance to be informality. We have moved away from old forms of elegance that prescribed rigid patterns of dress and propriety (and depended on inexpensive domestic service) to a more relaxed and easy kind of manners.

In contrast, however, there are signs that we have recently embarked on a more formal era than we have had for some time. More and more members of the communications and business aristocracies are having their clothes made in Savile

Row in London, where the tailoring is elegant, formal, and conservative. Shoulders are not padded, except imperceptibly, sleeves are slimmer, lapels are narrow. "In a word," the actor Clifton Webb said when asked why he has his suits made in London, "English tailors make clothes for gentlemen." (It is only recently that actors have come to be admitted to the rank of gentleman.)

But by no means all of the formality is conservative. The men's clothing industry, determined to make men as fashion conscious as women, is again reaping handsome profits out of formal attire. (When it is formal you evidently do not call what men wear "clothes"; you call it "attire.") A Philadelphia clothing firm that claims to manufacture 55 to 65 per cent of all "formal attire" for men in America says it has doubled its business in the last three years. The tuxedo, known to the more expensive trade as the dinner jacket, and to the French as *le smoking*, is not the conservative object it once was. For one thing it weighs about a pound and a half less than it did fifty years ago, and it can be bought in colors that haven't been seen on dressed-up men since the days of lace cuffs, jabots, and silk knee breeches. Indeed, the trade calls the colors "hues," and you can buy tuxedos in such edible tones as "blueberry," "strawberry," "grape," and "banana." This fruit-salad approach to formality is evident in men's shops everywhere,

but no more so than at Brooks Brothers of New York, traditionally known as a stronghold of the conservative and an institution as proper as a girl's seminary.

It must be apparent to anyone who thinks men dress in something of a uniform—and evidently most women do—that men's fashions are an elaborate set of contradictions and paradoxes. At the same time that men are becoming more informal they are also becoming more formal. More businessmen now buy work clothes than used to, and more who used to wear work clothes all day and a blue serge suit for dressing up now wear jackets and slacks—a sportsman's costume. Men who dress for the office in a modest way become peacocks on their days off.

There are both easy and solemn ways of explaining this paradox. One we have already mentioned—that bright plumage has always been characteristic of the male animal. Another is (and there is evidence for it) that the men's clothing industry has decided that men have been submerging their natural desires to show off and cloaking them in conservative suitings. "This cloak must be ripped aside," says a spokesman of the industry, "if wool manufacturers are to benefit from the great psychological unchaining that is stirring among today's male population." He further urges that the industry "fill the unsatisfied needs" of men and "glamorize and sexualize" their clothes. The solemn way to explain the new concern for prettiness is to say that in an age of anxiety, as our age has been called, we put on a gay façade to keep up our spirits.

But none of these explains—and so how does one account for?—the most recent paradox in male attire, the popularity of the charcoal-gray suit, the drabbest garment to appear as a man's costume since the early days of the industrial revolution when men, though they dressed their wives magnificently in tremendous crinolines, affected the solemn black of factory chimneys for themselves.

The charcoal-gray suit, so conservatively cut as to minimize the characteristics of the male figure, with sloping shoulders and a jacket that not only modestly conceals the waist but seems to exaggerate the width of the hips in a somewhat feminine fashion, is the costume of the successful and would-be successful businessman. It originated with the tailors who provided clothes for proper young men of the Ivy League colleges, with shops like J. Press in New Haven and Cambridge, and Brooks Brothers in New York. It is the most conspicuously inconspicuous costume devised for men in our time, and by its very conservatism it exudes an aura of propriety. It seems to say, "I am properly dressed for any place, any company, and any situation. I am modest, self-assured, and I have no need to show off. I do not need to substitute fancy dress for personality." It is a uniform that covers a multitude of uncertainties and a multitude of

platitudes, and it is worn with well-polished loafers or cordovans. Properly it is accompanied by a pink, gray, blue, or white shirt (sometimes with a starched collar and pleated front), and a regimental striped tie, slim knitted black tie or other conservative neckwear. Loud ties are out, but French cuffs with large cuff links are in. This is not a regional phenomenon. Charcoal gray and "charcoal brown" (whatever that is) dominate the men's clothing market. Not only expensive stores provide the expensive look; it is everywhere. It is on the streets of Dallas and San Francisco, of Chicago and New Orleans and Washington. It is even in Denver, which is normally about two years behind the fashions for men in New York.

The problem of telling one man from another is further complicated by fads that seem to dominate the country: "everybody" is wearing the new look, or "all men" are buying charcoal gray, or "all children" are Davy Crocketts or space men. It sometimes seems as though fads are all-pervasive, but they never quite are, even now when we are beleaguered by the moans from Upper Bohemians about "standardization." There are regional differences, though each year they become less evident. In Texas you will find echoes (sometimes unpleasantly hollow) of the state cattle tradition in the broad-brimmed Stetson and cowboy boots worn by men on city business. In Denver, where altitude makes the atmosphere rarer, visiting ranchers wear their pants tight and respectable businessmen go to work in loose slacks and sports jackets, though the Brown Palace Hotel insists that neckties be worn in the dining room. In Los Angeles there is a canyon as wide as a CinemaScope screen between the well-dressed downtown businessman and the Hollywood "creative" worker. The businessman dresses pretty much like his counterpart in Chicago or New York (except that he doesn't wear a hat). But, as an advertising man in Los Angeles put it, "In the cinema and TV set the motive is 'look the part.' If you can imagine the masculine counterpart to a mink coat and pedal-pushers, you can 'roll your own.' " Theatrical agents, on the other hand, are the very picture of Madison Avenue three-button, charcoal-gray elegance.

Some cities that are far from what are usually considered centers of fashion turn out sartorial sports. In St. Louis not only did Bermuda shorts recently become acceptable for casual wear, but men turned up at country club dances in shorts with black satin stripes, white dinner jackets with plaid cummerbunds; in Madison, Wisconsin, red Bermuda shorts turned up at summer dinner parties.

Ordinarily one might consider such costumes eccentric. Not today. As each year's clothes get fancier it becomes harder to tell the eccentric from the conventional, until one suspects that tomorrow's eccentric may be the man in a coat that matches his trousers. In Houston now you will find an

occasional vice-president of a bank wearing slacks and a jacket to work; you would never find such informality in a New York bank. In Chicago, I have been told (I didn't see it myself), a magnate of the stockyards turned up for a symphony concert in Orchestra Hall in riding breeches, patent leather pumps, a plaid shirt and a dinner jacket. My informant didn't say what kind of socks joined the breeches and the pumps. Fortunately for our rules of thumb there are always a great many people who are impervious to fads and stand somewhat aside from trends. They go their individual ways, untouched or only slightly touched by what "everybody" is wearing, the despair of the clothing manufacturers, who would like to keep them in a constant state of indecision.

While there are a few sartorial characteristics that distinguish one profession from another in this era, personality is more likely to emerge from details of haberdashery. Lawyers in San Francisco may tend toward tweeds, whereas West Coast doctors hanker for blue pinstripes, and actors everywhere (except the Clifton Webb types, who occupy what they assume to be an aristocratic position in the theatrical, or more particularly, Hollywood, world) have suits that are exaggeratedly broad in the shoulders and narrow in the hips. Mere ownership of a checked sports jacket or a charcoal-gray suit does not necessarily tell you anything about a man; millions of men own them. What he wears with the jacket or the slope-shouldered badge of conservatism, however, can tell you quite a lot.

Take the inhabitant of the intellectual pyramid, for example, or the would-be intellectual. His most dominant feature is his glasses, which in nine cases out of ten have black or near-black heavy frames that give him an owl-like look. (Actually the further up the pyramid you go the more modified you find these characteristics. In matters of appearance lofty position tends to lead to conservatism.) He plays his clothes down, as though he were above such material considerations. He wears black shoes and often a black suit, a white shirt and a dark necktie in a solid color. The points of his collar, uninhibited by pin or buttons, are likely to jut out sharply. He avoids hats, unless he is bald, but if he wears a hat it has an aged, beat-up look. Nothing about him has any sharp edges. There are Bohemian variations of this costume, the most obvious of which is a dark blue or brown shirt in place of a white shirt, but the Bohemian intellectual is easily distinguished from the Bohemian artist or hopeful actor.

The artist is likely to pick the individual items of his clothing because of their qualities of color or pattern—a checked shirt or a pair of *café-au-lait* corduroy slacks. But how he puts them together is of no particular concern to him. He cares less for the total effect than for the items, and he adds up to a sort of bouillabaisse, tasty but miscel-

laneous. The Bohemian actor in our day may, on the other hand, seem just as miscellaneous in his choices, but the items are put together for a single purpose: to create a theatrical effect. He is always quite obviously in costume, not in mere clothes. Following the tradition of the pre-Oscar Marlon Brando, he tends to dress tough rather than fancy; he carries his imaginary waterfront with him. His faded blue-jeans fit him like satin upholstery and his shirt is not open just at the neck—it is open. There is a sharp distinction between the little-theater actor and the one who has made Broadway or the big TV shows. Once he has made the big time, he stops affecting the romanticized version of the stevedore, washes his face, cleans his nails, and turns up looking like an exaggerated version of an advertising man in charcoal-gray suit and pink shirt.

Because a man is not an actor it does not mean he is any less interested in creating a personality for himself. A man's problems of dressing, now that the standard uniform of earlier days has been discarded, are not unlike a woman's problems when decorating her house. Both have to decide who they are, what public effect they want to create, what kind of society they live in, and with whom they are going to compete. Are they conservative? Are they adventurous? Are they eccentric? Do they run with the pack, and, if so, with which pack? Do they want to be thought of as tough fellows or good fellows? As smoothies or as lovable Teddy-bears? As dear old Charlie or sharp-as-tacks Mr. Think?

It is not difficult to sort them out, once they have sorted themselves out, though it would be extremely difficult, in most cases, to say how they make their living and to whom they owe allegiance. You will find, for example, that the lovable types affect soft tweeds that bag. Their pockets bulge with pipes and tobacco pouches; their neckties are moderate in color and rather conservative in pattern and as likely as not made of challis. They like flannel shirts and brogues and old snap-brim hats. You would not be likely to find them in either the new flat-top hats or the caps with a buckle on the back which are for the young and the hopefully Peter Pan-ish. Their clothes wear a comfortable smile.

Mr. Think, on the other hand, is always well-pressed, is likely to wear a dark suit cut not in the latest style but not out of date either. He pulls the knot of his tie rather too tight, and his neck has a chickenlike, pinched look in his sometimes starched collar. He never wears a double-breasted suit, always (except in summer) has on a waistcoat, and prefers French cuffs that he can "shoot" to emphasize a point of argument. His shoes are plain-tipped, black, and always shined. He wears a gray or black hat set squarely on his head and carries a furled umbrella (for possible use not for chic) whenever the morning newspaper hints at rain. When he is relaxing at home, he dresses as conscientiously

for the part as he does for his business role. He wears an all-one-color playsuit of slacks and short-sleeved shirt and canvas shoes, and he buttons the shirt at the neck.

Mr. Think's costume may vary from city to city, but his general air of gingerly meticulousness does not. In Washington (which he always refers to as The Nation's Capital) the flair has gone out of senatorial costumes along with the string tie, come-to-Jesus collar, and congress boots. In an administration by businessmen everybody dresses something like Mr. Think, and the dark suit is considered proper for all but the most elaborate functions. (It is possible that if the Russians hadn't refused to wear dinner jackets, the U.S. Senators would have; under the circumstances they cannot.) White shirts are the accepted uniform on the Senate floor, though the pale blue shirt is occasionally seen—partly, I am told, because some Senators want to look as though they had been invited to appear on TV (white shirts glare under the camera's eye).

Currently in New York one sees a diplomatic variation on Mr. Think, primarily because of the United Nations. The sartorial language of diplomacy has changed from something dapper to something solemn, and here again I suspect the Russians are at the root of it. The diplomatic Mr. Think's costume is a black suit and black tie; his glasses are black rimmed, and he inevitably wears a black Homburg and carries an attaché case. I have never been able to figure out exactly how far up the diplomatic career ladder one must have climbed to wear a Homburg, but I should think at least as far as third secretary to a delegation. This costume is also affected by intellectuals who act as management consultants to industry and by many foreign-trained psychoanalysts.

The genus of smoothies lends itself less readily to specific description; the symbols are less standardized and universal. The fop of the Edwardian era meant something rather specific as did the gay blade of an earlier time, but the present-day smoothie exhibits many professional and regional and financial variations.

A Los Angeles smoothie, for example, cuts a quite different kind of swathe from a Newport or Long Island smoothie, and a teen-aged one bears little resemblance to the middle-aged smoothie. About all of them there is, however, a sort of self-contained air of concentrated purpose, of an animal on the prowl. Grooming is extremely important, and their nails and hair undergo the most worshipful attention. They always carry combs and use them frequently in public, for their hair is likely to be on the long side. (There is something a little too fresh-air for them about a crew cut. Their world, they like to think, smells of musk.) There is a slight exaggeration about the cut of their clothes; the coat drapes fulsomely, especially if it is double breasted, and is buttoned at the bottom button. This has a tendency to

emphasize the width of their shoulders. If they are in the charcoal-gray set, the shoulders of their jackets slope like ski jumps; increasingly they button all three buttons on the front (a few now wear four-button jackets), they have an extra ticket pocket, with flap, and may even have buttons on their cuffs that unbutton. The double-breasted, pinstripe, dark blue suit and Windsor knot in the necktie worn with a rolling collar were typical a few years ago of the smoothies in the entertainment business. In an exaggerated form it has become the uniform of the young men who model them-selves after crooners. They tend away from loud neckties to knitted black ones, and they wear sports cars and con-vertibles as they wear their clothes—for effect.

There is, of course, something of the smoothie in every man. The urge to combine suavity with sex appeal manifests itself in surprising ways. There is the man, for instance, who considers a neon-loud necktie as sexually irresistible, a sort of advertisement of his malehood, a dash of daring in an otherwise drab monochrome of pale face and pale clothes and pale personality. There is the zoot suit and its current English counterpart, the Edwardian-inspired garb of the so-called "Teddy boys," who dress in tight jackets and peg trousers and wear embroidered waistcoats and frilled shirts. There is the current fad among teenagers for the leather jacket strung with zippers—diagonally across the front, on the sleeves and on the pockets. It originated with the motorcycle cowboys, and has almost become a uniform for juvenile delinquents. All of these are variations, or perhaps one should say corruptions, of the genus Smoothie. There is a name for the variation; it is Glamour Boy.

The men we have looked at so far all seem to be exaggerations of one sort or another, but the current tenor of men's clothes is in itself exaggeration. What about those men that women call "just nice, ordinary men," those amiable souls who exist more in the imagination of women and in ladies' magazine fiction than in the neighborhood? They are the uneccentric ones, the sensible ones, the grown-up boys, the ones who always pay their bills on time, who are as faithful as the dawn, as even-tempered as steel, good providers, good fathers, comfortable as an old shoe . . . somebody else's husband. What about them?

They cover themselves with just clothes—with what is acceptable in their "crowd" and at their age. They are the conservatives in pepper-and-salt suits and gray fedoras or in blue serge and gray felts with narrow ribbons, the Fuller Brush men, brushed to tepid respectability. Their socks are what their wives buy them and their neckwear first appears to them in Christmas wrappings. They are neat and well pressed; their shirts are white and lightly starched; their brown oxfords are polished, even though they turn up slightly at the toes. These men do not, above everything, want to be conspicuous, though they want to be thought of

and dictated by etiquette rather than manners did not concern them. If they choked in stiff collars and sweated in woolen waistcoats, it was part of the cross they bore without complaint, so long as they fitted the pattern and did not "make a spectacle of themselves." Now it is the average man who, his personality given wings, darts like a fruit fly from plum to raspberry to peach. He is an eccentric among millions of other eccentrics, but unlike the true eccentric he has a problem of protective coloring. He wants to be different but not really different. He wants to express his personality as he sees it, but he does not want to give himself away. He wants to be in fashion but he shudders at the idea of being fashionable.

The truth is that he wants neither to be mass produced nor lonely, so he seeks his solace in being some of both.

Chapter VI

The Part-Time Lady

THERE is probably no subject that consumes more journalistic print today than what is known as "the woman's problem." It is conveniently faceted with thousands of glittering questions and complaints, and there is an audience of untold millions of women who wear their problems like costume jewelry—big, gaudy, and more often than not simulated. The "man's problem," by comparison does not exist; you will find no books about men that are comparable to *Modern Woman: the Lost Sex* or *The Second Sex*, nor will you find magazine articles devoted to the plight of the male in our society. If he has a plight, it is assumed, it must be his own fault. The plight of women, on the other hand, would seem, if the amount of space devoted to it is a reason-

able measure, to consume the reading hours of more than half the adult population. The simple fact seems to be that the woman's problem is separate from the human problem, but that the man's problem is not.

It is not my intention to argue the merits of this situation; I have just devoted myself briefly, if not altogether sympathetically, to the male, and I would now like to turn my attention to an aspect of the female in America that gets very little attention. There is a good reason why it doesn't. It can scarcely be called part of the woman's problem; it can scarcely be called a problem at all. It is simply the matter of what, in our new society, is a lady, if indeed there is any such thing.

One evening not long ago I called to my sixteen-year-old daughter, who was doing her homework, and she came into the room where I was sitting.

"Do you know what a lady is?" I asked her.

"Gee," she said, "*now* what have I done?"

That wasn't the answer I expected, and it made me laugh. She looked surprised.

"That's not what I mean," I said. "When you think of a lady, who comes to mind?"

She thought for a moment: "I don't think I know any ladies."

"Oh, come on," I said. "Not any?"

"Well, maybe Mummy's a lady."

"What do you mean, *maybe?*"

"Well," she avoided my question. "Granny's a lady from the top of her head to her toes."

It took a few minutes to pin her down. She thought of none of her contemporaries as ladies; it was an ideal of behavior that seemed to be of no immediate concern; it had to do with older women, off there in the future somewhere.

If you were to ask the same question, I believe that you would find that it sets women, even young ones, slightly on edge. In our day it puzzles men, as it would not have a generation ago. The old concept of a lady as an upper-class, straight-spined, and rather useless (if ornamental) creature whose standards were social rather than human has fortunately disappeared.

I have asked quite a number of men and women what a lady is. I asked my secretary, for instance. She accepted the question amiably, if a little startled, and went about asking some of her friends. I trust my daughter's judgment where her contemporaries are concerned—up to a point. I asked her to ask her classmates what a lady is. I have also asked members of my mother's generation. I have asked my colleagues. I have asked my wife. There has never been a less scientific or more inconclusive opinion poll than mine, but it does, I hope, throw a glimmer of light on the position of women in our society, if not on the woman's problem.

My question was simply and abruptly: "What is a lady?" All of the answers started much the same way: "What is a lady? Why, a lady is . . . well, let's see . . . what *is* a lady? You know, that's a very interesting question."

That is as far as some people ever got. Most of my respondents, to use a pollster's word, launched on their answers and could not stop. Before pinning the ladies down, let me first give you a few broad generalizations that emerged from the answers.

A lady is nothing very specific. One man's lady is another man's woman; sometimes one man's lady is another man's wife. Definitions overlap but they almost never coincide. A great many women, I discovered, do not think of themselves as ladies; they are modest and they know themselves too well. On the other hand they expect to be taken for ladies by other people. Most men think of their mothers as ladies, since mothers in most cases set their sons' standards of feminine deportment. Teen-age boys are likely to divide all women over twenty into two broad categories—"ladies" and "babes." To most men in their twenties ladies are women over forty. To many working women (a category which here includes over-busy housewives as well as office workers) ladies are women who have the time to be immaculately groomed, to smell good, and to sit and listen while others talk. To most women, and this I suppose is significant, few women have time to be more than part-time ladies; the larger part of their time is spent picking up after other people—children, husbands, or bosses.

As you can see from these generalizations the word "lady" has no exact meaning today, but it does contain consistent overtones of admiration. It is a state of grace that women would like to achieve and that men would like to be able to take for granted.

My researches have led me to several rather out-of-the-way sources, and some rather obvious conclusions. The first and unavoidable source merely proves that all women in America are ladies. You have never heard of a lady going to the women's room. It is always vice versa. It is "ladies' day" at the ball park. Women who used to be called "sales girls" are now "sales ladies." There are also "ladies of the evening," which seems to me to be pushing the word a little further than is absolutely necessary. I have checked the listings in the New York (Manhattan) telephone book, and I have found that ladies out-number women almost two to one. Under *women*, for example, I found such organizations as Woman for President & Other Public Offices Inc. and Woman's Apparel Shoulder Pad Assn Inc. Under *ladies* there was a brighter note: Lady Joy Undies, Lady Bountiful Salon, and most interesting (and rather puzzling to the historically minded) the Lady Godiva Undergarment Corp. One of the soundest, and also most progressive, labor unions

in America is the ILGWU (International *Ladies* Garment Workers Union), and surely the ladies who make the garments also wear them.

Before we make an assault on the bastion of the contemporary lady and try to define her as she exists today, I should like to try to put the American lady in context. That is, I should like to give you some background of the lady as she has been regarded by somewhat earlier generations.

When Harriet Martineau, the first distinguished newspaper woman of London, visited America in 1834, she arrived at a time when a good many Americans were putting on airs. It was the first era of the common man; that is, it was the first opportunity that the common man had in America to become as uncommon as he pleased. Andrew Jackson was President, and he had brought with him to Washington a new kind of society that made the old aristocracy turn pale with shock. "Respectability" became everybody's quarry, not just the quarry of the few. It was then that all American women became ladies. Miss Martineau was surprised to hear a preacher say from the pulpit: "Who were the last at the Cross? Ladies. Who were the first at the Sepulchre? Ladies." But she was even more surprised when she visited the jail in Nashville and asked if she might visit the women's cells. "We have no ladies here at present, madam," the turnkey said. "We've never had but two ladies, who were convicted for stealing a steak; but as it appears that they were deserted by their husbands, and in want, they were pardoned." The ladies, it appears, had a woman's problem.

But there were ladies everywhere. "By 1845," Dixon Wecter wrote in *The Saga of American Society*, "New York boasted a Ladies' Oyster Shop, a Ladies' Reading Room, and a Ladies' Bowling Alley elegantly equipped with carpets and ottomans and girls to set the pins." And a writer in 1855 (a woman) complained of the number of "females in their ambition to be considered 'ladies'" who used their hands entirely "in playing with their ringlets, or touching the piano or guitar." John H. Gregory, an Irish prospector who struck gold in Colorado in 1859, threw down his pick and cried, "Thank God, *now* my wife can be a lady!"

But there was another aspect of the position of women in America that is more important, and to foreign visitors, has always seemed very strange. This is the deference accorded to women here. One traveler remarked: "From the captain of a western steamboat to the roughest miner in California, from the north, south, east, and west we hear but one voice. Women are to be protected, respected, supported and petted." That was a century ago. Just recently another Englishman, Sir Harold Nicolson, commented in his book *Good Behavior* that he could not understand "the position of power and privilege claimed by, and accorded to, the

American woman." He wrote: "It is not merely that American mothers and grandmothers expect and obtain a level of worship comparable only to that established among primitive matriarchal societies of the Malabar coast. It is that American wives assume a contemptuous attitude towards their husbands, whom they exploit economically and to whom they adopt an attitude of cultural superiority."

These are hard words, but they are not unfamiliar ones. The position enjoyed by women in America came about for good and sufficient reasons, even though those reasons have worn out their usefulness by now. In frontier America there was a shortage of women. Short supply leads to hoarding and protection, and often to the assumption that the object that is hoarded has remarkable virtues. So it was with women in America. In the dust-blown and fly-blown villages of the prairies in the last century a woman "was absolutely safe both in fact and in reputation," as James Truslow Adams wrote in *The Epic of America.* "The conditions of frontier life often compelled a man to be away from home and perhaps take refuge for the night in another house where the man was also absent. For the sake of protection of each man's own wife, a sort of unwritten law came to be universally and absolutely observed. No man would think of approaching an honest woman, and so rigidly was the rule observed that even when men and women, perhaps absolute strangers to one another, thus spent the night under the same roof, no whisper of scandal would be breathed because it was felt there would be no foundation for it." There is no longer a shortage of women in America; women outnumber men today, but the fact remains that the tradition is so ingrained that men act today as though the shortage had not been alleviated.

It is not my purpose to engage in an argument about whether American women take advantage of men or not. I am talking about ladies, which is, or ought to be, a quite different subject, and I do not want to lose my historical theme quite yet. It was really men who made American women into ladies, and not women themselves, by putting them on an elaborate pedestal. It was a convenient way not only of flattering them into thinking that they were very special, but of lording it over other men. The American man's dream in the last century was to make enough money so that his wife could be as useless as possible, to surround her with servants and luxuries, to hire somebody else to bring up her children, and to house her in something like a full jewel box. In other words to make her into a lady he could be proud of and not have to worry about. If he could do this, he considered himself a success. He left all cultural matters to her, all matters of taste and education, while he pursued the dollars for her to spend. The result was, according to Henry Adams, that "the American woman of the nineteenth century was much better company than the

94 · · ·

American man." And according to Henry James, "Nothing . . . is more concomitantly striking than the fact that women over the land—allowing for every element of exception—appear to be of a markedly finer texture than the men. . . ."

It would be interesting to know what Henry James would say about American women today; it would probably not be greatly different, though the American woman has changed tremendously in the last half century and so has the American man. The American man has concerned himself a great deal more with matters of culture and taste and the American woman has given up the pursuit of being a lady. She decided some time ago that there are much more interesting ways to spend her time and employ her talents than cultivating the feminine graces and charms with all their subtleties for their own sake. She not only went to work in a man's world, and finally captured her political equality, but she gave up her long skirts, flexed her muscles, cut her hair to look like a boy, and took up men's sports.

So much for history.

"A lady," said Sinclair Lewis in a debate, "is a woman so incompetent as to have to take refuge in a secluded class, like kings and idiots, who have to be treated with special kindness because they can't take it."

It was not so very long ago that Lewis said this, only about fifteen years, and yet it is already as out of date as bloomers on a girl's basketball team, and smacks of that same era. Today there are no secluded classes, and there is no place in our society for the woman who "can't take it." The problem of the woman who wants to be a lady today (and I think we can assume that in some sense every woman does want to be considered a lady) is how to be a lady and, at the same time, all things to all men, women, and children. To her role of glamour girl, career woman, mother, house-wife, chauffeur for the children, Den Mother for a litter of Cub Scouts, one must also add the battle of the supermarket, her avidity to hold her own culturally and to do her share of "good works." Her life is a full, if not necessarily a rich, one. Lillian Day said in *Kiss and Tell* that a "lady is one who never shows her underwear unintentionally." The problem of the busy modern woman almost seems to be when she would ever have time to show her underwear on purpose.

Today's woman is expected to maintain her poise at the same time that she is pulled to the north, south, east, and west by demands which she has, in fact, asked for. It was women, not men, who inaugurated the feminist movement that was intended to liberate women from their domestic and matrimonial bondage and to give them a chance to be not just chattels but whole people, to realize their intellectual potentialities, and assume responsibilities. It is true, as we have already noted, that they have shunted some of their womanly jobs onto their husbands. However, it re-

mains their province to be women, for, as James Branch Cabell said, "No lady is ever a gentleman."

This does not contradict the assertion that part of the lady's problem today is how to cope with gentlemen on their own ground. More and more women are not only in business but are assuming positions of authority which have traditionally belonged to men. They are, of course, executives in department stores and advertising agencies; they are also, according to the *Wall Street Journal*, increasingly sought out by corporations for "high calibre sales jobs." The demand for women trained in the Harvard Business School (under the watchful eye of Radcliffe College) far exceeds the annual supply of bright young things; they might, without pushing the word unnecessarily far, be called the "ladies of the morning." The fact is that the ambitious woman of the last century worked at being a lady, for that was how she gained influence and position for herself and advantages for her children. The ambitious woman of today works at being a part-time man. The time she has left over is devoted to being a lady, and sometimes to being that part of a woman which is a drudge.

It is for this reason, I believe, that the term "lady" is taken for granted by the older generation, who remember when as few women as possible tried to be anything but ladies. It also explains why my generation (the middle one) looks upon the term as having connotations of snobbishness, of pretentious gentility, and of being unwilling to face the facts of economic and social change. The young are so far removed from their grandparents that they know the word "lady" only as "ladylike," and they therefore distrust it, as they very well should.

My secretary, after pursuing the investigation I suggested to her, put it this way: "The twenty-year-old group seemed startled and confused when asked to define a lady. Those in their thirties have definite ideas about what a lady does or doesn't do (and each rather diffidently assumes she is one); those over forty are shocked that one should have to ask."

We still have not defined what a lady is today, but while almost everyone I asked has a definition of a lady, a great many of them seemed uneasy about using the word at all. For all its being bandied about as a general substitute for the word "woman," it is old-fashioned. It is all very well to speak of "ladies," meaning any woman over twenty, but when you call a woman a lady, smile.

One evening at dinner recently I asked an editor of a very well-known woman's magazine what a lady is, and she said, "I hate that word." To her it implied class consciousness. You may have noticed that in the title on the cover of the *Ladies' Home Journal* the word "Ladies" is in such small type that it is almost unnoticeable. Not long ago that same magazine published an article called "What Makes

Grace Kelly Different?" and in it Jimmy Stewart of the movies is quoted as saying: "Grace is good. She has class. Not just the class of a lady—I don't think that has anything to do with it—but she'll always have the class you find in a really great race horse." It is, it appears, better to be compared to a horse than to a lady.

Her Serene Highness, however, does seem to have had some standing as a lady in a good many eyes, especially the eyes of the young, who, I have found, put Audrey Hepburn (especially for her performance as a princess in *Roman Holiday*) in the same category. Why? Largely because they both have a somewhat aloof and reserved dignity which, while it gives the impression of friendliness, seems almost to defy intimacy. By their presence and persons they make it quite clear that one should keep his distance and mind his manners. Alec Guinness said of Grace Kelly in the same article in the *Ladies' Home Journal* in which Jimmy Stewart mentioned the horse: "Around her, one finds oneself being careful of language and things like that." One friend whom I asked to define a lady said: "A lady is a woman to whom you apologize when you tell her a dirty joke." And Don Marquis once wrote: "There are three kinds of limericks: limericks to be told when ladies are present; limericks to be told when ladies are absent but clergymen are present—and limericks." It is interesting that in many eyes Grace Kelly should have tarnished her attractions as a "lady" when she married Prince Rainier. In the nineteenth century rich American mothers, like Mrs. Bradley Martin and Mrs. William K. Vanderbilt (who captured the Duke of Marlborough for her daughter) were in constant pursuit of European titles for their marriageable daughters, and though many people were amused, some of them very wryly, they also took it for granted as one of the eccentricities of the upper classes. When a movie "queen" who is also thought to be a "lady" marries a minor prince with all the attendant folderol today, one almost feels that it should not be mentioned in the presence of ladies without an apology.

But who are the ladies in whose presence one does not say such things? Not so very long ago there were many convenient rules for the behavior of a lady and many aphorisms to describe her. They do not apply today, but in 1900 a lady lived by such tidy rules as these:

A lady never raises her hands above her shoulders in public.

A lady never smokes. Only actresses and foreign women smoke.

A lady never crosses her knees.

A lady never uses lip rouge.

A lady never calls a new acquaintance by her Christian name, unless requested to do so.

A lady never engages in argument at a social gathering.

> *A lady always sits with the base of her spine against the back of the chair.*
>
> *A young lady never ventures out unchaperoned in the evening, even when she is with a group of her contemporaries.*
>
> *A lady never goes into the street without her hat and gloves and she never walks rapidly.*
>
> *A lady never discusses her children, servants, clothes, ailments, or house except with her intimates. These are the five forbidden "D's"—Descendants, domestics, dress, diseases, and domiciles.*

Any book of etiquette of the day listed a great many "ladies never" but such easy commandments do not apply today. The question of how to define a lady is now a different matter for different generations. The young define her in one way, the middle-aged in another, and the older generation in still another.

When the young speak of their contemporaries as "ladies," there is likely to be venom in their hearts. They mean prissy. They mean "genteel" with its common overtones of affectation. They mean being snobbish and upstage and too proper and too clean and too fussy. But when they apply the word "lady" to their elders the words "charming" and "gracious" come easily. Clothes play an unsurprisingly important part in their concept of a lady. "Modest, unpretentious clothing," one sixteen-year-old said, and another:

"Above all a lady is neat." Still another said: "A man may not want to spend his life with a lady, but he certainly enjoys them as refreshing balm." This same girl added (and I catch only a glimmer of what she means): "She may not have morals, but she has high ethics." The teenager's need to be listened to is evident in the remark, "A lady is interested in what you say," and her optimism in ". . . being a lady is something that comes with maturity. It's a quality that comes unconsciously out of a person's character." There seems to be a consensus among the teenagers that "it's hard to get to be a real lady, especially in modern society." The most constantly used adjective was "calm" or its equivalents "at ease" and "poised." Finally a lady is "sincere."

When you move up a decade or two and inquire of the middle-aged you find different adjectives which betray different attitudes. You find that "self-sufficiency" and "perceptiveness" become important. Intelligence also counts for more. "A lady," one lady said to me, "is a woman who creates an atmopshere in which people behave their best." And another: ". . . a woman who can rise to any situation." Worldliness and sophistication count for a good deal. "A lady is a woman who has accepted her disciplines." Not bad. But perhaps more important: "There is no trace of snobbishness in a lady." Another woman said: "I discovered early that you could go anywhere in New York if you dressed

and behaved 'like a lady'—it was like an invisible shield."
And a man said: "A lady is a well-adjusted but not over-
adjusted woman." Freud was bound to get into the middle-
aged attitude somehow.

When you come to the older generation another dimen-
sion is added; the definition of a lady includes "breeding."
It is a word little used now because of its class-conscious
overtones, but it was common enough thirty years or so
ago. We have dropped it just as we have dropped the word
"common" as it used to be applied to people who were loud
and rude and pushed themselves forward. We have also
dropped the word "vulgar" in this same connotation.
"Breeding" was meant to be the antithesis of "common,"
and it implied that it took several generations to make a lady
or a gentleman. Lady to the older generation not only had
implications of social standing but of idleness; women
worked and so did "ladies in reduced circumstances," who
displayed "gallantry" in so doing.

To us this seems to be an attitude reminiscent of nineteenth-century novels of manners, of the days when ladies
had fainting spells and men had legs but ladies had limbs.
Our notions of what a lady is have changed and are still
changing. It is a better word than it used to be. It no longer
bears any relation to idleness or the command over the
services of others. The implication of social parasite has
gone and so has every trace of snobbishness. No lady is ever

rude or overbearing to the people who serve her, for she does not think of them as her inferiors. The wives of the men who occupy the positions at the top of the social pyramids may look down on the wives of men who rank below their husbands, but they do not regard them as lesser ladies than themselves. A lady has no position; she has only her self-esteem. "The great secret," Shaw says in *Pygmalion*, "is not having bad manners or good manners or any other particular sort of manners, but having the same manner for all human souls: in short, behaving as if you were in Heaven, where there are no third-class carriages, and one soul is as good as another." He also says: "The difference between a lady and a flower girl is not how she behaves, but how she's treated."

If our society is becoming increasingly classless, then Shaw's "great secret" of manners becomes increasingly apt, and the only definition of a lady that applies to our egalitarian concept of society is, it seems to me, this: *A lady is a woman who makes a man behave like a gentleman.*

Chapter VII

What Has Succeeded Success?

W E LIVE in an age of ink blots and I.Q.'s. Our intellects and personalities are reduced to percentiles and "profiles"—classified, categorized, analyzed, and summarized in a thousand different ways. We select our college students, assign our soldiers and sailors, decide the careers of boys and girls, and try to discover what normalcy is by questionnaires and multiple choice tests, by putting pegs in holes and by running the results through an IBM machine. We are constantly on the search for abnormality at the same time that we distrust our standards of what is normal. We cherish the "well-adjusted" individual at the same time that we hurry past the question "well-adjusted to what?" One can scarcely get a job anywhere, even as a salesgirl (or lady) in an Oklahoma City department store, as a momentarily displaced career woman of my acquaintance tried to, without being subjected to a three-hour intelligence and personality test. (My friend did not get the job; the interviewer said she had an "artistic temperament" and couldn't get rid of her fast enough.)

My distrust of the validity of questionnaires is deep and abiding, but I am almost always fascinated by the results of those I happen to see, and some of what I have to say in this chapter is based on what I hope is accurate observation and some, I confess, is based on questionnaires.

Not long ago I was asked by the editors of *Mademoiselle* magazine to shuffle through a stack of questionnaires that they had sent to several hundred young women in their last years of college and several hundred others who had recently graduated. The questionnaires were intended to pry out of these young women their notions of success—in college, in jobs, in marriage. Unlike many questionnaires that I have examined these seemed to me agreeably civilized both in the questions asked and in the ways in which they were answered.

Some of the young ladies were wistful, some defiant; some were puzzled, quizzical, romantic, and some, but only a few, had a glint of hard ambition. A few were blasé or

smug. But all of them seemed to be frank. "Private faces in public places," W. H. Auden wrote, "are wiser and nicer than public faces in private places." The private faces that looked up at me from the questionnaires were, many of them, wise and nice, but I scarcely recognized them. The meaning of personal success, not very long ago thought to be "the attainment of wealth, fame, etc." (Webster's) had changed. The look in the eyes seemed different from the look I was used to seeing in the young. Wealth and fame, it would seem, are not worth the bother and the sacrifice; the aim has become well-roundedness.

Success has become a matter of neither impinging too insistently on the world nor letting the world impinge any more than is essential on one's self. The dream is of comfort and not excitement, of security and not prominence, of developing as many of one's potentialities as possible in a modest way without letting any one of them run away with the others. A job is a way of meeting "interesting people," of keeping amused, but it must not be all-absorbing. "I think definitely that a job should not consume your life," wrote a girl from the University of Texas. "It should be one in which you are interested and which enables you to lead a well-rounded life." Another girl, from the University of Wisconsin, echoed this: she said that she was interested in a job, "but only to the extent that it wouldn't interfere with a well-rounded social life."

A Surfeit of Honey . . . .

The devotion to well-roundedness appears to go further than just ambition for oneself. It applies equally to ambition for one's husband. Few of the private faces seemed interested in marrying a man determined to get to the top of his profession, who by hard and persistent work would push back the frontiers of his chosen field. They were thinking of his happiness and of his health, and they cast both in the setting of relaxed weekends—the picture of thoroughly barbecued bliss. "I want my husband to be ambitious but not dangerously so," wrote one college girl, and another said, "I don't want him to have such a high executive position that it would ruin his health or personal relationships with his friends or family." Throughout the answers there was a constant identification of work and achievement with ruined health, lost friends, unhappiness. It was associated with trampling on other people who are also on the ladder, with having no time for the children and working incessantly over weekends. "The college girl's picture of a Successful Person," commented one of the young editors of *Mademoiselle* who had spent a good deal of time over the questionnaires, "seems to be a combination of a bore, a bastard, and a battered-and-broken adventurer."

And money? Money is all right so long as you can buy happiness with it. A great deal of money, young women believe, can only be acquired at the sacrifice of virtue, sincerity, children, principles, and well-roundedness. "Just

enough to get along comfortably," seems to be the goal, though the meaning of *comfortably* varied considerably from answer to answer. Most of all they want their husbands to be happy in their jobs, and not to break their necks or their hearts trying to get rich. "No job," wrote one girl, "should encroach on relaxing time." As you might expect, the young wives who answered the questionnaire that was sent them took a more lively interest than the college girls in the quantity as well as the quality of their husbands' pay checks.

The family is, of course, the ultimate measure of success —its solidarity, its community of interest, the well-being of the children. In this money plays a secondary role; it is time that matters—time for the husband and wife to putter together, to play with the children (three or four of them), to have neighbors in (nobody wants to entertain "business friends" if she can help it), and to indulge in what are known as "outside interests." The goal for marriage, like the goal in college, seemed to be characterized by a desire not for Phi Beta Kappa but an "all around good average." The key word is "adjustment" and the place is "to one's environment." Adjustment to one's environment is, I believe, the opposite of the conquest of it.

But these are generalities. Specifically, adjustment means a series of compromises between one's interests and one's ideal of the good life; environment means a good deal more than just place. First of all, environment means the family, and adjustment to it means marshaling all of one's other interests to making the family a success. It means supporting the career that your husband has chosen with enthusiasm tempered with sweet reasonableness, lest he overwork or overworry. It means seeing that one's children are given every opportunity for healthy and well-adjusted (there's that word again) lives. But environment also includes the world of the mind, and the concept of well-roundedness insists on the maintenance and development of one's intellectual interests. There must be time for reading, for concerts, for active participation in local educational and political matters. One should be "well-informed"; that is, one should be able to discuss international affairs with the same confidence that one discusses gardening, baseball, or Bartok.

The good, well-rounded life seems to be lived as much out of doors as in, for it is assumed that all men would rather be on the golf course, in the garden, on hikes and picnics, or in boats than anywhere else. This assumption is fortified by the belief that whatever interests a husband must also interest his wife and she must participate with the fullness of her heart, limbs, and mind. It seems as though life were to be lived on the college elective system with a major in homemaking and a minor in physical education. The life of the mind must be cultivated, but its activities

are somewhat like those necessary but peripheral courses elected to complete the essential credits for a degree in well-rounded living.

To ignore the electives is to be a failure; it is to fall short of the ideal of success. How can you get along with all sorts of people (one of the primary qualities of being well balanced) unless you are alert and well informed and yet free of the lopsidedness so often associated with overconcentration? It is a life, obviously, that to be lived successfully has to be lived furiously in order to get everything in, and yet its essential quality is that of seeming relaxed and ready for anything. Wife, mother, pal; well read, well adjusted; tasteful, tactful, tolerant; active, patient, intelligent. And a lady besides? How does anyone have time to be well rounded?

If this is the success the young women of today are pursuing, they are embarked on careers of sweat and toil. While they are reading they will be worried about not being on the tennis court or at a PTA meeting, and while they are indulging their own predilections, they will be looking over their shoulders to see whether their taste manages at the same time to be personal and yet uneccentric. They must be concerned with expressing themselves without overstating their case; they must be creative without offending anyone—which, let it be said, is all but impossible. It is very likely to be the well rounded who are most offended.

Is there, do you suppose, any real risk of developing a

criterion of success that is based on well-roundedness? A great many well-rounded young women summons up for me a large bunch of hothouse grapes—lovely to look at, plump, smooth, carefully protected from the crankiness of weather, and tasteless. Pebbles in a stream are also well-rounded; so are the vowels in the mouth of an elocution teacher. What is the likeness of the well-rounded male, the mate desired by the well-rounded female?

First of all he is affable, friendly, and trustworthy and he tries to be all things to all people. He gets on easily with everybody, everybody, that is, who is also well rounded and even with a few who are not. He is conservative in his tastes for furniture, foods, entertainments, and women. He is conscientious, does his duty by his community and, when called upon, by his country. He never gets caught off balance (neither, incidentally, does a ball, which is also well-rounded), and he changes his mind slowly because he likes to see all sides of a problem. He is a man whose principles are not easily shaken, though he knows how to give a little here and take a little there; he recognizes that compromise is not without virtue if it is used for virtuous ends. He prefers the *status quo*, but he does not deny the processes of evolution. This tends to make him conservative in his political opinions, but he is not a reactionary. He is a middle-of-the-roader. He is a natural do-gooder within the realm of his convenience and of what he expects the opinion of his circle

of friends to be. He is not, however, going to risk his position in the community by espousing an unpopular point of view. He pushes no frontiers back. He does not get "burned up" about anything, except, possibly, those things that threaten his position in the pyramid of society in which he lives or that might endanger his property values or the well-being of his family.

Someday I should like to meet the well-rounded man I have just described. He must be a rare and remarkable specimen. I doubt if he exists at all; he is merely a literary figment, the kind of man one discovers only by trying to strike an average from the answers to a questionnaire. He is not an individual; he is just a generality. He is a statistical meatball, the lean and the fat all ground together.

But there is evidence that the meatball is not unrelated to reality. David Riesman in an article in *The American Scholar* told of a study of Princeton seniors that had been made by *Time* magazine. Interviewers had asked the students what they thought their lives would be like in fifteen years. "No life in the ulcer belt for me," one of the young men said, and another said, "Why struggle on my own when I can enjoy the big psychological income of being a member of a big outfit?" The theme of well-roundedness emerges as clearly from the Princeton seniors as it did from the *Mademoiselle* girls. One young man who plans to be a lawyer said (and Mr. Riesman after some initial doubt decided that the young man wasn't trying to pull the interviewer's leg): "I'll belong to all the associations you can think of—Elks, VFWs, Boy Scouts and Boys' Clubs, YMCA, American Legion, etc. It will keep me away from home a lot. But my wife won't mind. She'll be vivacious and easy with people. And she will belong to everything in sight too—especially the League of Women Voters. I won't marry her until I'm twenty-eight, and so when I'm thirty-six we will have only two of the four children I hope for eventually. We'll be living in an upper middle class home costing about $20,000 by then, in a suburban fringe. . . . We'll have two Fords or Chevvies when I'm thirty-six, so we can both keep the busy schedule we'll have. But in addition to this public social life, we'll have private friends who don't even live around Toledo—friends with whom we can be completely natural and relaxed. That's where Princeton friends will be very important."

Mr. Riesman, who doesn't take the results of the *Time* survey too seriously, says of the young men: "The career they want is the good life, for which their corporation or profession serves as the good provider. These men already know they won't be president—they wouldn't want the job with its unpredictable demands, its presumptive big city locale, its disruption of family and recreational life."

The temptation to make a generation fit such a formula leads to alarm and distrust on the part of those who do not

belong to it and disgust and boredom on the part of those who do. But this brief composite portrait of a generation's ideas of success is not entirely without validity, and if it seems to be without any very sharp edges we must remember that generations are also without edges; they are not compartments; they are merely what we mark off for the sake of convenience on a continuous line.

Actually the changes in ambition and in the concept of success are not only changes in where people want to get but also in how they want to get there. They do not want a peak but, as Riesman says, a plateau on which to live. They want to proceed up a road that has protective barriers on either side; they want to go step by step up the corporation ladder, some faster than others, of course, but with a sense of security about the climb. There is more kudos, because there is also more security, in a man's being part of a large and nationally known corporation than part of a small one. There seem to be fewer men and women who want to desert the road and high-tail it to a higher peak that can be reached only over rocky terrain. The dream of the young family is to move not only up the road of career but to move from suburb to suburb. Many young families today start life in the mass-produced suburbs where houses are all alike and, it is said, there is only one class since everybody makes about the same amount of money. Their ambition is to move as soon as they can afford it to a slightly older and better-established suburb where each house has a little more land and is not the image of the house next door, and so on to older suburbs and more land and bigger houses. At each step there is a slightly larger and more expensive car, more "appliances" in the kitchen, perhaps better schools for the children and with luck private schools. You will, as we have seen, find a different notion of the good life set about with different kinds of accouterments among the Upper Bohemians, but the theme of security underlies their ideas of success as well. The gamblers of our time are the artists, and those other adventurers who go it alone, the heavy thieves.

But let us go back a couple of decades and see if we can uncover a few of the reasons why words like well-roundedness, security, and adjustment have replaced words like ambition, success, and achievement in the vocabularies of many young men and young women.

Many of the parents of those who are now in college or who have recently graduated were married in the twenties —the era of the so-called Lost Generation, of the boom that seemed as though it would never end, of Bix Beiderbecke, and the 4 per cent income tax. The world had been saved for democracy once and for all by the First World War, and anybody could save himself by following the formula of Dr. Emil Coué. All you had to do was to repeat over and over each night before you went to sleep the magic words

"Day by day in every way I'm getting better and better"; your psyche took care of the rest. Young men stepped out of college into jobs that paid them handsomely; they bought stocks on margin and doubled their money as though by divine providence. The world gave them a living and bath-tub gin and exaggerated notions about prosperity. Then the crash caught them. A few jumped out of the windows of office buildings; some just could not pay the mortgage on the house; a good many found that what they thought were steady jobs with promising futures were no jobs at all. About the only things that went up after the crash were the woman's waistline and the bosom; they were almost the only natural resources whose value had not been over-estimated.

Faith in money as a goal to which to devote one's entire energies was destroyed. Money turned out to be ephemeral just as surely to those who had put their life's savings aside in "sure things" as to those who had made money out of money on the market. Success when measured in dollars be-came a hollow thing, a faithless mistress not to be followed or flirted with. The war had saved the world for democracy and democracy was broke. The intellectuals were called in to tinker with the economic machinery, and see if they could get the motor going again. A few wanted to tear the motor down and remodel it according to a nineteenth-century blueprint devised by a man named Marx; others

wanted to patch it up, give it a shot of high-octane plan-
ning and see if it would not begin to hum again on its own.
Panaceas became the order of the day.

Those who graduated from college in the thirties found
that there were no jobs looking for them; they had to dig
for anything that would pay them a few dollars. They
found that their elders were taking stock not only of the
economic machinery but of human machinery as well. People became "social problems" and their "security" became
a political issue. The social security program was enacted
into law in the middle thirties, and by the forties labor
unions were concerned with "benefits" (for health and old
age and such) and not just with wages. Education was
going through its "progressive" pangs, and the adjustment
of the child to the group became more important than what,
if anything, he learned from books. Measurement of the
intellect and the personality by tests and the establishment
of "norms" for behavior became a routine that almost every
school child took for granted. The secret of the results of
tests (usually kept from parents and children alike) gave
the young a feeling of being prejudged and an uneasy sense
that their elders knew, as though by mind reading or magic,
what their destinies would be. To be exceptional or over-
gifted in any one direction was to be suspected of being
susceptible to maladjustment to the group. Child psychol-
ogy had come into its own and competition among children

was minimized; the verbal report took the place of grades in many schools. Competition, it was believed, hindered the development of the "whole personality," and a premium was put on creativeness of whatever sort. "Creative" became a cliché and almost meaningless; every school child wanted to be creative (or at least his teachers wanted him to be, however matter of fact the little fellow was), and every graduate from school wanted a creative job. Discipline went out of fashion; if a child did something he shouldn't, his parents "explained it to him." The emphasis was on moderation, adjustment, and "well-roundedness."

Then the world turned out not to be safe for democracy at all. Democracy had to fight for its life. The planners with their doctrines and panaceas and the young men and women who had been brought up by "permissive" parents turned into fighters along with everybody else. They believed that once Fascism was licked we could settle down again to solving our economic and social problems and to building reasonable lives. What we got was prosperity, the threat of Russia, an entirely unfamiliar set of problems, and a whole new freezer full of mores, idols, and aspirations.

This alone might explain the present cautious concern of the young with security and well-roundedness. But there is another and equally important cause, as Pangloss could prove, for this effect. Their parents' generation, which had at first wrung its hands over its failures, soon began to forget the lessons it had learned in the depression. Once more they saw visions of an ever-expanding economy and they began to dance on the dikes that, they were confident, could withstand any floods that might threaten prosperity. They slipped back into old habits of complacency and acted as though this were, after all, the best of all possible worlds. Once again they seemed to think that they had all of the answers and that a beneficent government run by beneficent and practical men would protect them from all evil. There were cushions and crutches everywhere. But there was something a little unreal about their euphoria, something a little too smug about their self-confidence that seemed to betray a distrust of themselves and their faith.

Their laughter has become a little too loud, their jokes a little too shrill. They make an uneasy vibration in the air. The young cannot help but feel it.

Chapter VIII

Good Times!

Optimism: The doctrine or belief that everything is beautiful, including what is ugly.

AMBROSE BIERCE

SIXTY-FIVE million Americans have jobs, more than ever before, and the "national personal income" is over $300 billion. This figure presumably means one thing to economists and something else to the rest of us. It inspired the Secretary of Commerce to say to reporters that he is filled with "cheery optimism."

. Tiffany & Co., jewelers of New York, recently advertised in *The New Yorker* a diamond necklace "of simple elegance" for $168,300, "including federal tax." The tax on the necklace would be $15,300.

In an age in which everything, including prosperity, is two-toned, the manufacturers of the Continental car, which sells for about $10,000, and is all one color, urge customers to feel "the thrill of being conservative."

"Business is healthier than I've ever seen it," a Boston engineer said not long ago. "But one thing that bothers me is that my children have never had to fight for anything." The engineer, who now runs his firm very profitably, had gone desperately into debt during the Depression.

"Some folks claim it's the katydids," a Midwestern corporation executive said to a *Wall Street Journal* reporter, "but I know it's different. It's the sound of all those debts amortizing."

The Secretary of Labor, who did not quite see eye to eye with the Federal Reserve Board, believed that the sound of debts amortizing was a healthy, delightful obbligato of prosperity.

When Dr. Ernest Jones who, you will remember, said that tranquilizers couldn't cure politics, was asked for his impression of America last spring, he used a single word, "Extravagance!" Dr. Jones's last visit to America was in 1929; it felt much the same to him in 1956.

But whatever happens to the smile on its economic face, America, we may be sure, will never look again the way it

did in the dreadful days of the thirties. It simply cannot. It is a different place. It is lived in by different people. There are forty-five millions more of us now than there were in 1930—enough people to populate the United Kingdom in those days. How we *might* look if we tumbled from our pinnacle of prosperity is anyone's guess.

We do not have to guess, however, at how we look at this moment, and the picture, I'm afraid, is not altogether heartening. It is true that we have conscientiously gone a long way toward distributing our riches among ourselves and toward helping others to take advantage of their own resources and ours. We have reorganized our social system with less plan than purpose—the route was certainly not carefully charted, though we have known in general where we wanted to come out. We have arrived at a far more equitable relationship between men and women, even though we are still accused of being something of a matriarchy. The position of men is a less artificial one—even if gaudier to look at—than it used to be in the days when Father posed as family emperor but Mother ruled the castle. There has been a drawing together of family interests, a redistribution of some family functions, and a clearer understanding of who is responsible for what. All that, I cannot help but think, is good, or if not yet good at least better. But only the most dyed-in-the-wool Pollyannas, the most direct descendants of Dr. Pangloss, could look about them and say that this is, after all, the best of all possible worlds. Superficially (I hope it is only superficially) the Baron's castle is something of a shambles. The sad and undeniable truth is that prosperity has made monkeys of far too many of us.

As New Yorkers say, leave us face it. People are getting ruder. Service of all sorts is deteriorating. Juveniles are getting more delinquent. Traffic is becoming impossible. Advertising, no longer motivated by the need for making converts, affects an air of studied lunacy. Black eye-patches triple a shirt manufacturer's business. Beards sell tonic water. Wolfhounds sell vodka; sheep dogs sell rum; men in flannel suits drinking on the hind quarters of white horses sell Scotch. Botany Brands uses a female model with four arms (like an Indian Shiva in sequins and opera hat) to display items of men's wear. Presumably in a period of prosperity two arms per woman are not enough. A foreign car distributor promotes the Jaguar as "schizoid." Monty Woolley and others pose indoors with open umbrellas for a vermouth manufacturer to show how dry they keep their martinis.

The line not only forms on the right; it stays there. Long lines of bank depositors wait at two open wickets while five others are closed and unattended. "An airline can save money by having fewer people taking reservations," a traveler said to a reporter of the *Wall Street Journal*, "and in effect I pay the difference because it costs me more time to

get a reservation." It takes longer to get the fifteen miles from the Newark Airport to New York by bus than it takes to fly to Newark from Washington. Mail service from New York to London (by air) is often faster than from Wall Street to Park Avenue (by man). A press agent arrived at the Conrad Hilton Hotel in Chicago late one night to find that the suite he had reserved was occupied by a flock of turkeys left over from a turkey growers convention. City buses, a friend of mine commented, have the herding instinct. There will be none for ten minutes and then five will come, like elephants holding each other's tails.

No wonder that almost every month sees the publication of another cookbook for sufferers from ulcers or hypertension (the "salt-free diet"). The *Harvard Business Review* publishes a study of "The Executive Neurosis." A social anthropologist at Harvard says that "social mobility" (or social climbing) on the part of women generates anxiety in men and anxiety generates ulcers. In Vienna Professor Erwin Stransky says that women "drive men to earn more and more money to satisfy their desire for luxury" and that this results in nervous disorders among businessmen. The Metropolitan Life Insurance Company reports that "more men than women are hospitalized for mental disorders in the United States. . . ." Doctors are worried about the increasing unauthorized use of tranquilizing drugs like Serpasil and Miltown. The dean of the Psychoanalytic Clinic of Columbia University said on March 17, 1956: "We live in an age of enormously increasing anxiety, despite the fact that 'we've never had it so good.'" He blamed this on "the absence of a ceiling on aspirations." According to the Metropolitan Life, "People in the farm states of the Midwest [from which one hears few cries of prosperity] live longer than those in other areas of the United States. . . ."

Jacques Barzun writes in *Harper's* of young concert artists who are paid $250 for a concert: ". . . it is not even possible after paying one's expenses to make a living, which means that the piano tuner is better off than the pianist he serves." A Senate subcommittee on juvenile delinquency (Estes Kefauver, chairman) reports that it has found in the movies increasing emphasis on "sadism, brutality, and violence." The *New York Times* reports that "Stravinsky Adapts His Firebird, Seeking Juke-Box Fame, Royalties." Magazines of the "confidential" variety outsell most others on the newsstands. R. H. Macy & Co. and *McCall's Magazine* are whooping it up for "togetherness," whatever that is. Maybe it has something to do with a statement by Dr. Florence H. Kluckhohn to the Commission on the Education of Women of the American Council on Education. She said: ". . . women are functioning concurrently in the component roles of mother-housewife, career woman, glamor girl, culture bearer, and status symbols of their

husbands or fathers." How much more together can one woman be than that?

"Of all the groups in America," William H. Whyte, Jr., of *Fortune* wrote in a book called *Consumer Behavior,* "none is so ill-equipped emotionally as the new white-collar class to adjust to a severe economic downturn, and if our society has an Achilles' heel, this may be it."

The *Wall Street Journal* quoted a professional worker at strike-bound Westinghouse: "Man, you don't realize how closely geared your standard of living is to your income until you've missed a pay check. Frankly I was shocked to find out how quickly we felt the impact."

A woman who lives in a $35,000 home in the New York suburbs and whose husband makes a salary of $15,000 a year said to a reporter: "My husband gets paid the first of the month, and the last few days we always run a little short—I had only a dollar, for emergencies, and no gas." She had to leave her green DeSoto station wagon in the garage.

The "bad debt" business is booming. "We're having the best year in twenty-four in this business," said the manager of the Heller Collection Bureau of Warren, Ohio, to a *Wall Street Journal* reporter in 1955. Another man in the same business in Des Moines whose volume had jumped 100 per cent in a year said, "My business is so good it has me worried."

A Surfeit of Honey . . . .

A young man in his thirties, a suburbanite, said in a confidential mood: "I always tell myself when I find myself getting another bank loan: 'If that banker is a big enough fool to lend it, I'm a big enough fool to borrow it.' And in the end if it gets to the point where they want to take my house away from me, well, what is the bank gonna do with it?" This fellow makes $17,000 a year. His wife says: "You don't order your life against catastrophe." And he says, "I've got to live this way; I'm caught up in it and can't seem to let go."

Almost everything he buys he buys "on time." Out of his monthly income (after taxes and such) of $1,100 all but $35 is committed.

A headline in the *Wall Street Journal* on the day after income taxes were due last year read: "Many Americans Rush to Banks, Pawn Shops, Borrow Cash for Taxes./Taxpayers Pawn Television Sets and Wedding Rings . . ." It added: "A Wife's Solution: Divorce." The article contained this item: "The manager of a Pacific Finance Co. office in the Los Angeles area recalls this case: 'A woman borrowed $400 from us the other day to pay her income tax. She has a substantial income of her own and her husband works, too. She told us she's going to have to get rid of her present husband—her fifth—because he's making too much money.'"

You can buy anything on time: a husband, a wife, a

wedding, and a honeymoon ("wedding spending is rising, say merchants in the field, even though the number of marriages per year has fallen in recent years"); automobiles (a "$100-a-week truck driver spends a year's pay" on a $5,511.60 Cadillac); house furnishings, of course. And a car dealer in Miami offered a share of stock in General Motors to anybody who bought an Oldsmobile from him; another dealer offered a free trip to Paris "complete with a tour of some Parisian night spots."

You can even buy the illusion of time itself: ". . . all makes of cars except Cadillac," a Stamford, Connecticut, attorney said in defense of a client who had been pinched for speeding, "are built with 'fast' speedometers to make drivers think they are going faster than they are." The client, who was "something of an expert on speedometers" (he had patents on a couple) accused the police of having fast speedometers in their cars. The judge found him "not guilty."

The multi-million-dollar do-it-yourself boom was responsible last year for 600,000 accidents. About 15,000 amateur carpenters smashed their thumbs or otherwise did themselves in, and 57,000 people banged themselves up climbing around the gutters and troughs of their roofs. Another report says that the cost of doing-it-yourself (which was, of course, initially a means of saving money) has risen so much that many people can no longer afford to do it themselves.

The rate of suburban home building has swallowed up golf courses, woodlands, and almost every other sort of property that makes it worth bothering to live in the country. Suburban communities, short on long-range plans, have been selling their birthright. "The builders by now," said Nathaniel H. Rogg, economist for the National Association of Home Builders, "have pretty much exhausted the improved land left over from the premature subdivisions of the 1920s, and there's no place for them to go but further out." (The Government recently offered twelve small islands in the Florida Keys for sale.) Forty million people, according to the *New York Times,* have moved out of the cities "in recent mass migrations," creating a whole new set of problems for welfare services of all sorts. "I'm all in favor of gracious living," said the Dayton City Manager last year, "but this exodus to the suburbs is causing problems for the central city, too. On one of our streets alone, the traffic of suburbanites to and from work has been increasing about 30 per cent a year. It cost us $500,000 just to repair the street."

The trouble with prosperity is too much money, of course. Successful businessmen fret about making too much too fast. The threat of "the next higher bracket" hangs over their heads like a scimitar on a golden thread. When things get really tough for them, they have nothing to do but sink

oil wells, an activity on which the tax laws smile benignly. ("When a fellow is in my income bracket," said a Midwest industrialist whose annual income is over a million dollars a year, "he automatically goes into the oil business.") Less successful businessmen worry about all the people in hock to them and all the people they are in hock to, because in a period of prosperity nobody dares not to seem prosperous. A New York businessman apologized for turning up at a meeting last winter. "If you're not in Florida at this time of year," he said, "your creditors get worried." It is not solvency in such a time that matters; it is the appearance of luxury—the command over the fruits of other people's labor.

What happens? People get to thinking that they had better pluck the fruit while there is still time, and having plucked it, they happily squirt its juice into other people's eyes. They worry about getting more money until they get it, or more goods until they can find a way to put off the day when they will have to pay for them, and then look around and find that their friends have everything they have. Everybody's name becomes Jones. But most of all, plucking the fruit gives them a convenient and well-sloganed reason for not thinking. Their pattern of behavior is known as "supporting the national economy." They can be satisfied that their role as consumers is essential to the national well-being. No one ever did his social duty with so little apparent strain or inconvenience.

No one, on the other hand, ever got so worried about "the meaning of life." Ask the clergy. Ask the psychiatrists. Ask *King Henry the Fourth, Part One*—"They surfeited with honey and began to loathe the taste of sweetness, whereof a little more than a little is by much too much." Ask your best friend. Ask Bridey Murphy.

Put in its rudest terms, prosperity produces not only plenty but curiously empty values and a national uneasiness. It produces strange kinds of personal economic competition in which symbols like the automobile and the freezer represent a burning desire for status. Cars get gaudier; hi-fi sets get hi-er, beer can openers become mink-bearing, open fields are swallowed up to make future slums, slums are torn down to make parking lots; pastures become drive-in movies; drive-in movie operators provide heaters so that one does not have to desert his status symbol even in winter. Artists and architects, writers and musicians worry about hits and their spoonfuls of gravy rather than about their art. Everybody, or nearly everybody, gets tense about the unknown—about flying saucers and foreign relations, about tomorrow, especially about tomorrow.

Obviously I exaggerate.

The kinds of behavior I have described are by no means everybody's behavior. Behind the extravagances there are restraining hands. There is the concern about financial

security that is so strong among those young who have their hearts set on being well rounded. Among many of the middle-aged there is a strain of disbelief, perhaps not nearly skeptical enough, that the party cannot go on forever and that the hangover will be mean. Among the old who live on fixed incomes and whose dollars have shrunk like woolen socks there is a justified cynicism: what, they would like to know, is all this talk about prosperity?

There is, contrary as it may seem, something to be said for depressions. (There is also something to be said for heat waves, droughts, floods, wars, and metropolitan blizzards.) There is nothing to be said for the evils depressions produce, for empty stomachs and ruined homes, for bread lines and broken families, and the terror of not having a job. There is also nothing to be said for the bully boys in their brown shirts or the Huey Longs or the Father Coughlins who baited the desperate with promises of plenty in exchange for subservience, for circuses when there was no bread. But prosperity has produced its own bully boys, trading on fear and suspicion.

There is a great deal to be said for the climate that a depression produces, a climate in many respects more productive than prosperity—more interesting, more lively, more thoughtful, and even, in a wry sort of way, more fun.

I do not advocate, as who would?, another depression, but to put our present era in a perspective which it blatantly

Stir Customer's Wrath," or "Call to Repairman Brings Only Headaches to Many Householders." You did not have to threaten to sue the man who put linoleum in the kitchen because he did such a slipshod job and then refused to meet the specifications you were paying for. You could catch the eye of a waiter. People who knew how to do things were proud that they did. The mechanic repaired your car; he did not half repair it so that you would have to bring it back next week, and a dealer did not mark up the price of a new car so that he could give you what seemed like a magnificently high price for the old one you were turning in. Almost no one was subservient, but almost no one quite dared to be lofty either. Manners were more relaxed and more friendly, as they are whenever there is a crisis; when everybody is in the soup, no one worries about sitting above or below the salt. In a depression competition works to produce maximum efficiency and utility of services and products to attract the consumer's dollar—the most for your money, not the most display with the shoddiest workmanship for the money.

But more important a depression not only gives people time to think, it *makes* them think. Men and women are not only more ingenious about entertaining themselves, they are more thoughtful about work, with the result that they get more personal satisfaction from it. The challenge is a real one, not one inspired by snobbery or "social mobility" or the fear of losing face. It is a dampener to frivolous ambition, but it is a spur to real ambition. It taxes the imagination (a tax which, to be sure, many people find it harder to pay than a tax on net income), and it produces ideas which are more than just notions. In a depression a bad idea is a luxury that cannot be afforded, though, as it happened, we had to afford some all the same.

A depression is, in this sense a hot war. It brings to bear on essential problems of survival the best hopes and the best brains that can be rallied. But it has this over a hot war— and over a period of prosperity: the survival of everybody is equally important. It took time, but we finally learned that there were no human expendables. The artist was as important as the munitions maker, the ballet dancer as important as the pilot, the housewife as important as the brewer— no more, no less. The problem was not one of power but of the person, not of the future but of the present. The problem became not how to lick somebody else or be licked by him, but how to restore personal well-being and dignity. There's a tremendous difference.

It is easy to extol the virtues of a past era even when the nostalgia is partly painful. I am not one to say that pain is good for the soul, but contemplation is. In some respects we are still living on the fruits of our enforced contemplation during the depression and what it did for the arts, for pol-

itics, for business, and for science. We turned the arts loose by giving all artists some sort of chance to survive for a little while. We took time to do basic research in the sciences because we were not in too great a hurry to do "development." We took time to develop a new kind of architecture, but we did it sparingly with time to consider our mistakes. We did not, as we do now, build furiously, repeating our hasty mistakes thousands of times over—acres of identical dwellings, avenues of identical glass-faced office buildings, thrown up in the manner of the latest fad because there is no time to think and little inclination to consider the pleasure of the individual. Curiously at the same moment when it is the public-relations façade that counts most, business produces an architecture that looks as though it had on it the dead hand of social service. But business is now living on the architectural ideas of the 1930's as contentedly as it is living on many of the restrictions and safeguards that were placed on its affairs by a government it considered hostile and fought tooth and nail.

Our depression was obviously no great flowering like the Renaissance in Italy in the fifteenth century, but it had some of the artistic and economic earmarks of that earlier depression. "Italy, the earliest and most brilliant artistic renaissance," said Professor Robert Sabatino of Yale at a symposium at the Metropolitan Museum four years ago, "felt the impact of economic recession most heavily. Its condition resembled somewhat that of . . . New England after 1929."

It would not be entirely surprising if the days of the depression were looked back on many years hence as the beginnings of America's flowering as a mature nation. In any case it is those who remember that evil can come to a flower whose roots are not tended, and watered, and fertilized, however gaudy the blossom, who will keep it alive. Those who learned to garden in drought do not forget the watering can.

But what about those who have been brought up with the garden in full and furious bloom, when some of the blooms are real, and some are wired to the stems? What about the victims of prosperity? What about the members of the expense-account society who live in somebody else's lap on wealth that does not really exist until they spend it? What about the young wife who stays at home with her children and her freezer while her husband spends the company's money wooing customers at "21" or the Stork Club? What about the children who are jammed into old schools because communities cannot get steel to build new ones since the state legislature would rather vote funds for super-highways? The automobile business gets first call on steel, and the motorist first call on the public pocketbook; school children were better off in the depression. Their

parents took more responsibility for them. What about the young families who are picked up every year or so by the corporations which control their destinies and set down somewhere else, families that do not dare to grow roots? What about the members of unions whose welfare funds are plundered by gangsters dressed as men in gray flannel suits?

What is all this uneasy concern for security in the midst of plenty? Most of the rest of the world heartily dislikes us because of our prosperity and the generosity which we can afford and the largesse we like to dispense. Why do they distrust us? Why, at the same time that we seem to be smug, do we so distrust ourselves? Why do we suspect that we are always outguessed and outmaneuvered by the Russians, outplayed and outpropagandized? Why in the world community do we act like poor little rich boys, all dressed up in our best clothes, with our faces scrubbed—and nobody wants to play with us?

There are many answers to these impertinent but by no means unnecessary questions. We change so rapidly that none of the answers, however, is likely to be valid for long, whatever truth it may have for the moment. In the last decade and a little more we have replaced fear with anxiety in the Baron's castle, and for that we can be thankful. When we were afraid, however, we did something about it—sometimes bold, sometimes timid; sometimes silly, sometimes wise. Now that we are anxious we seem to fret and fiddle.

But we must bear in mind that the castle has undergone in an astonishingly short time a very considerable renovation. We have swept out a good many old and worn-out pieces of furniture and relegated others to the sub-cellar. We have reorganized the servants, filled the kitchen with new equipment, put the gentlemen in new raiment, and given the ladies a more dignified position and a great many new responsibilities. We have reordered the factions within the castle, got rid of the old ruling class and elevated some new aristocrats to positions of eminence. But we have not settled down to keeping house. It is as though all of the furniture were still crowded in the middle of the rooms. It is going to take us a while to put the furniture where it belongs and to get the weeds out of the garden, which is a tangle of blossoms and fruits and tares. Of one thing we can be quite sure: the castle is never going to look again the way it did when we moved in. We are quite a different lot of people from the old inhabitants with quite different ideas of what makes the good life. We know that the drawbridge which we once could pull up and so isolate ourselves from the rest of the world is now down for good, and that some of the clouds that linger on the horizon are of our own making and are far bigger than a man's hand.

"All that is very well," as Candide said to Dr. Pangloss, who was prattling about the best of all possible worlds, "but let us cultivate our garden."

Set in Linotype Janson
Format by D. F. Bradley
Manufactured by The Haddon Craftsmen, Inc.
Published by HARPER & BROTHERS, *New York*

women—and why shouldn't it, now that men spend so much of their time on housework? So the clothing trade is fancying up the names of materials to catch the male fancy. "No more blue or pink or green," said a shirt manufacturer, "Now we pique a man's interest with Adriatic blue, Genoa lemon, Amalfi green, Sicilian peach, Valencia vintage, Sorrento mint, and even blanc white." He goes still further— "Moulin Rouge, Batiste, Pan Am Piqué, Sheeracle, and Oxfordian." He promotes the "Ivy look" (its trademark, a buckle and strap at the back of caps, trousers, Bermuda shorts) and wide hat bands with the bow in the back. He contends that men are "exhibiting excellent taste by coordinating colored shirts with suits, ties, socks and jewelry."

One cannot help but wonder about an age in which a man faces the day by deciding whether or not he will slip into a simple little Oxfordian three-button and a Valencia vintage with French cuffs or if, this morning, he will settle for Moulin Rouge or a "tailored sport shirt with a stand-up oriental collar." The change that has come over the extremes of men is far less surprising than the change that has come over the mean. There have always been men who enjoyed foppish and elaborate costumes and those who cared so little about clothes that any decent covering would do. Most men, little concerned with fashion, were content with a neat and inconspicuous costume, "suitable to the occasion." That the design of their clothes was inconvenient, uncomfortable

seems to lack, let's compare the productivity of the last depression with the present prosperity.

The Depression (it can mean only one thing to my generation—the years between 1929 and the war-inspired boom of the early 1940's) was temperate. Helter-skelter, sky's-the-limit ambition seemed silly. Nobody worried because his neighbor had a fancier car or a bigger house that cost more to heat. If he worried (and he often did) it was about essentials not frippery, about food and not whether he could satisfy the maw of the deep freeze, about how to get to work and not about the personal command of a two-hundred-and-fifty-horsepower rolling palace glittering with tinsel, about a warm coat, not about Mrs. Jones's mink-dyed muskrat, or Mrs. Upper-Jones's sable. Dreary? To some people, surely, but to many quite the contrary.

People were more friendly, less suspicious of each other, and went out of their ways to help. They felt strongly about national issues and worked hard and talked long about them. They had time to read (and to think) because reading was inexpensive; they had time to talk to each other because they did not see any way to interpose gadgets between themselves and their friends (no television), and they played games together because games cost little and lasted long.

You found in the papers no such headlines as you find today about "Tactless Store Clerks, Bungled Repair Jobs,